MAGGIE:
the dog who changed my life

MAGGIE:
the dog who changed my life

A Story of Love

Dawn Kairns

iUniverse, Inc.
New York Bloomington Shanghai

MAGGIE: the dog who changed my life
A Story of Love

iUniverse books may be ordered through booksellers or by
contacting:

iUniverse
1663 Liberty Drive
Bloomington, IN 47403
www.iuniverse.com
1-800-Authors (1-800-288-4677)

ISBN: 978-0-595-47435-6 (pbk)
ISBN: 978-0-595-48746-2 (cloth)
ISBN: 978-0-595-91712-9 (ebk)

Printed in the United States of America

For all the homeless pets;
may you find your forever homes.
For all animals;
may your spirits be seen as the expression of spirit that you are.
For Maggie,
who opened the doors to my heart and intuition.

"They're here to guide us, to walk us through life as a reminder of what we're all here to learn: what unconditional love really is."

John Edward in a
November/December 2001 *Best Friends Magazine* interview

Contents

Acknowledgments

With deepest gratitude to my husband Tom for your unending support, both with this love story and on our life journey together. You always found the time to edit, offer valuable feedback, and help me through my computer glitches. Thank you, my partner and best friend.

To my parents, for always loving me and giving me the means to make this dream a reality.

To Anne Wilfong, my good friend, for your title idea and for those memorable hikes to Blue Lake. For holding my hand during Maggie's surgery. For letting Maggie be your guide.

To Judith Laird, my special friend, who stood by our sides on our darkest days and guided us through. Thank you for recognizing Maggie's incredible presence and for being so present with us at a time too uncomfortable for many to handle.

To Bridgette Chesne, the Humane Society of Boulder Valley (HSBV) shelter manager, for taking the time out of your busy schedule to immerse yourself fully in this book and offer your heartfelt comments and suggestions before I went to press. Thank you and HSBV for all the animals you rescue and find homes for. Your creative programs are a guiding light for shelters and dog guardians alike.

To Ethan Watters, for your coaching direction and expertise. For truly hearing in my words on these pages that this indeed is a love story.

To Glenda Denham, for giving us the gift of magic that Maggie was.

The names of some of the people and places
in this book have been changed.

Introduction:
Once in a Lifetime

Once in every dog lover's life, if you're lucky, that special once-in-a-lifetime dog comes along. You know this relationship is golden, a gift from the spirit world. You have found a soul mate. Animal and human spirits are inextricably intertwined, and you know there will never be another dog that comes close to the presence of this one and the bond that you share. For me, Maggie is that dog.

You know it when it happens. You think a thought and your dog responds. She knows what you're asking of her, even though you never trained her to do it. You recognize that your communication is beyond words, beyond training. How do you explain it? You peer into her eyes and know you are looking into the depths of a loving, advanced soul. You may wonder, as I did, who *are* you in there?

When Maggie and I are out hiking, running errands, or just hanging out being "girlfriends," I meet several people who have loved and lost such powerful relationships with their canine companions. They recognize that magic between Maggie and me, for once you experience it with your dog, you can't miss it when it appears before you. I see the longing in their eyes, the painful missing, and the ache of irreplaceable loss.

"You just made my day," one man wistfully tells Maggie when she greets him at the coffee shop.

Sometimes I see this man keep his distance, and he just nods at me—as though it's too unbearable for him to touch the pain of his loss at this moment. I imagine his own precious memories with his dog dancing before his eyes.

"Enjoy every moment you have with her," the gentleman at the coffee shop tells me.

I do enjoy her every moment. I know the day will come when I will walk in his shoes with that mournful longing, when I'll be forced to learn to live with her absence. But to know it intellectually and to live it, I would later find, have nothing in common. That day, as far as I am concerned, is so far in the distant future it doesn't even exist in my awareness.

As a child, I was taught that animals were inferior to humans. We were superior to *all* life on Earth. This teaching was inherent in both culture and religion. Maggie helps me challenge that belief. She shows me over her lifetime that she is an intelligent, emotional being with a huge presence. I learn to respect her as a being who I share this planet with—a different being—not a lesser being.

Chapter One
The Gift of Magic

I am windsurfing with a group of fellow wind seekers at the Boulder Reservoir. When I meet Tom, we bend each others' ears regarding our current failing relationships. Our connection is immediate, as is our trust.

I find myself easily attracted to Tom. He is in great shape, with well-defined muscles. Where nature skimped on the hair on his head, it made up for in chest hair. His sapphire eyes emit a constant twinkle. His immense charisma makes him appear larger than his size. I am surprised to see him standing only an inch above my 5'3" when he stands next to me. Tom is funny and laughs easily. His manner is friendly and open. He loves people, brings them out, and helps them shine. When I talk, he listens well. I don't just pay attention to how he treats me. I watch him with both his male and female friends. Not far beneath the surface of his playfulness, he is genuine and loyal. Once Tom is your friend, you know you can count on him. Even before I fall in love with him, there is a sense that the world is right when he's around.

It is the best kind of relationship. Good friends turn into lovers. Tom and I are married on June 30, 1990. At thirty-seven, I am living with a man for the first time. The package includes his two sons, almost eighteen and twenty years old. Tom Jr. was away at college, so we barely know each other by the time he is living with us for the summer. Scott was still in high school and much more interested in girls and partying than spending time with his dad and his new wife-to-be.

1

Although they are kind and open to me, they are still trying to put the pieces together from Tom's divorce from their stepmom of twelve years. I am a stranger to them, as they are to me. And here we all are, suddenly thrust under the same roof as a blended family.

One dinner with the boys is so much like another. Conversations consist primarily of teenage banter between Tom Jr. and Scott. Then Tom's fifteen-year-old stepson Jeff is added to the mix one night each week. Three conversations buzz at once. Yet I recognize little communication exchange. What am I missing? Must be a guy thing. Tom and I seem merely on the sidelines.

At times, the chatter borders on crude. I hear "ho" repeated by all three of them when they refer to girls at school, and I cringe, as a member of the female sex myself. I finally inquire, "So, does 'ho' mean 'whore'?"

The buzz stops. Dead silence. All eyes are on me. Then they look at each other. One of them mumbles, "Ah yeah." The conversation shifts. Just for a few brief minutes. Although this is pretty normal interaction for teen boys, I feel it's a teaching moment crying to be utilized. After all, I am a woman, used to *meaningful* conversation. I didn't grow up with brothers, so this is really foreign. I watch and wait for Tom to step in, to guide them in communication and social skills. But instruction on how detrimental such labels are to females does not come; nor does coaching on the importance of listening, responding to, and engaging others. As stepmom number two, I don't feel it's my place to jump in to mold personalities at this stage of the game. I have no shared history with these young men yet, nor any bonds or commonalities, which build the foundation for trust and rapport. I am the newcomer to this family system, and I feel like an alien.

Scott taps on my office door after dinner, looking sheepish.

"We don't really mean anything when we say that stuff," he says apologetically. He must have sensed my discomfort. He does seem the most sensitive of the three boys.

"It's just not respectful to refer to girls that way, Scott. It's hard for me to hear."

"I know," Scott admits, looking at the floor. "It won't happen again."

"Thanks, Scott. I appreciate it."

And it doesn't happen again. When the boys start their "ho" bantering, Scott nervously interrupts with, "Hey, guys, do we really want to talk like this?"

At times, I discuss my concerns with Tom in private about the seeming lack of responsiveness among the boys in their communication. He occasionally interjects a comment to them, but I think they sense that Tom wants to be "one of the guys" with them. I think he knows their trust in him is shaken from his recent divorce. Chancing conflict with them is too great a risk for him.

In the midst of this sea of men, I am an island. I'm accustomed to the more intimate conversations I have with my female friends. Although Tom and I connect well, a macho energy prevails in the family arena. I sense their "tough-guy" walls, erected against the pain of living through two divorces. I don't know how to reach them. I wither on the vine. I am thankful for Shanna, my thirteen-year-old orange-and-white tabby. She is the link to my past. To gentleness. I long for a deeper connection in my life. Little do I know it is waiting for me just around the corner.

I love children and always assumed I would have my own. I adore my niece and nephew, Heather and Brad, and I feel like their second mom. Even though I moved to Colorado in 1977 and they remained in the Midwest, we spoke on the phone and visited each other regularly. At age twenty-four, I adopted a "little sister" through Big Sisters of Colorado when I moved here. Brenda was twelve. Now she is a mother of a teenager, and we remain in touch today. Kids were just a part of my life.

Yet even with what seems like a natural maternal inclination, I'm not sure I actually *picture* myself with children. I perceived my own mother as unhappy in her role. I grew up at a time when society didn't seem to value motherhood. That had a huge impact on me. I sensed that Mom felt trapped, and I never wanted to feel that way. Freedom was essential to me. I grew up during the women's liberation movement, singing along with Helen Reddy to "I Am Woman." I focused on getting myself through college and developing my career. Travel and adventure have been high priorities. So has personal growth. Being an idealist, I've been determined to have my life make a positive difference in the world. There were a plethora of people and causes crying for help. It seemed to me that once a woman had children, home life and family became almost a sole focus. That was all she had time and energy for. Without consciously realizing it, I wasn't making room for children in my vision of contributing my resources outside of home.

I suspect I'm a little afraid to have children. I came from a fairly dysfunctional family background. Part of my own healing was to create healthy boundaries. My mother was very obsessive-compulsive and controlling. For years, rather than call Mom on her difficult behaviors, the rest of us danced around her. We dealt with it by talking about her among ourselves. I wish we could have handled it more directly. Did I unconsciously fear that children would bring out my own neurotic behaviors and I would be criticized like Mom was? I realize now how unfair we were to her, yet Mom wasn't exactly approachable.

My father was the one who went out into the world and returned with funny stories and a sense of joy. He whistled while he gardened and fixed anything that broke around the house. He couldn't wait to hunt and fish. Dad's curiosity was peaked when he merely studied a rock. I wonder if I attached his happiness to not being home raising children, to his freedom to come and go. I adored my father. I also got the subtle impression from him at times, usually in jest, that what he was doing in the work world outshined my mother's work. I took that in on some level.

What seems to matter most is to passionately and authentically give the love that lives inside of me back to life. I don't believe having my own child is the only way to a fulfilling life. It's one potential way of creative expression—a very powerful means to love, give, and grow—but not the only way.

I'd been single a long time; long enough to be somewhat set in my ways. I never dreamed I'd be starting a family at thirty-seven years of age. I can go either way at this point. However, I do want time with my husband first.

"Since I was twenty years old, my life has been geared to support my family. My three kids have been my priority," Tom shares over dinner in Summit County. We went up to stay at his condo for a weekend getaway of hiking and biking in the mountains. "I'd like to retire someday and travel more. If we have children, I'll be focused on getting them through college. Then I see no end to working."

Tom's feelings are important to me. He is a certified public accountant and financial planner with his own practice in Denver. He's been very successful at doing corporate tax, but he pays the price in stress.

"What if we have another child like Scott?" Tom expresses a realistic fear. Scott had not been the easiest son for him to raise, and he still poses a challenge. He became hyperactive around age four and argued and pushed the limits with Tom in a persistent way his other boys hadn't. Scott struggled, and still does, to get through school. He often quits his jobs and usually believes he has been wronged somehow. Taking on personal responsibility has not been his forte. He loves to party and drink; in fact, a drinking problem is surfacing already. His mother, Tom's first wife is an alcoholic. But we are certain he'll outgrow it.

"Just think, we can be grandparents someday," Tom ventures. He is forty-two years old and ready for some freedom. The idea of starting a new family scares him. I understand that.

His feelings tip the scale for me. I have several close married friends without children. It makes not having children a more natural direction than if all my friends had kids. And so it is that Tom and I agree that a canine baby is the *only* newborn we will have together.

It isn't an either/or situation. They are two entirely separate issues. We will get a dog whether we choose to have a child or not. I had an intense love for animals, even as a child: dogs, cats, rabbits, and pigeons—I had and adored them all. But dogs were my passion. The neighborhood German shepherd, Flash, scared some adults in our neighborhood with his bark and size. Yet we were buddies. He waited at the end of my driveway for me to get off the school bus, and we played and wrestled together in our front yard. When I was in my troubled teens, I often thought out loud while walking with Sandy and Taffy, our beagles. They were good listeners and wouldn't tell on me.

So, a puppy it is. We decide in August 1990. Glenda, my friend and former landlady, tells us before our wedding that it will be her gift to us. We are surprised and touched by her generosity. She knew I missed living with her black Labrador, Axie. Tom had lost his black Lab, Otis, in his divorce. So the breed isn't a question.

"I really want a female to balance the abundant male energy in this house," I tell Tom one evening as we lay in bed reading.

"I'm okay with that," Tom agrees. "Male dogs roam more, anyway."

I am so ready and excited to have my own dog to connect with. I had dogs as a child, but they were different. Randy was the family dog. I dearly loved Dad's beagles. I had the pleasure of feeding and walking them, but they were *Dad's* hunting dogs.

It's almost Thanksgiving when Glenda calls. "I got the name of a good breeder in Denver from Axie's breeder. They just had a litter on October 21."

Our very own puppy has been born! She is out there waiting for us to find her. I can't dial Desperado Labradors fast enough to make an appointment for us to see the pups.

Choosing our own pup is a first for both Tom and me. The two of us drive to the breeder's home on Thanksgiving weekend, anticipating. Although Scott lives with us, it's more that he sleeps in our house. School, work, and his social life occupy his time. Tom Jr. already returned to the University of Northern Colorado (UNC) campus, working at his part-time job in Greeley. When the boys are here, they are more like our roommates at this point. At their ages, as you might expect, Tom's sons have little involvement with our day-to-day household. Since our new dog will be here much longer than either of them will, we don't consider them part of our decision process. This puppy is for Tom and me to raise, train, and be responsible for.

Joan and Paul Barnes lead us to their backyard that looks like it has seen a few litters of puppies. The patchy grass is badly in need of being reseeded. Then we see them. Five black and two brown balls of fur bob happily on the ground. Tails wag. Eyes twinkle with light and life. Bodies bounce into each other. Tiny teeth nip in play. A palpable joy surrounds us.

"They're adorable!" I exclaim. Tom's face melts.

We squat and invite these angelic balls of fur into our arms. One by one, tiny black and brown pups tumble over our feet. Nibble our fingers. Tickle our faces with their soft, pink tongues.

"How do we choose?" Tom wonders.

To help us more easily pick our black female, Joan removes the males and chocolates and places them in a small pen. Four black wiggly creatures surround us and vie for our attention. Gradually, their interest in us fades—except for one bright, smiling face—the one with a tiny white patch on her chest. Soul pours through her eyes. This precious one waddles in and out under my coat. Her tail wags nonstop. She circles Tom and comes back to me. Chubby paws land in my lap. A warm tongue touches my chin. Soft brown eyes peer into mine. Away she goes to roll with her siblings—but not for long. She comes back to us again. I know she is our girl. We already belong to each other.

I look at Tom. "Who is doing the choosing here?" he laughs.

The decision among the three of us is unanimous. Indeed, she is already living in my heart. This is our first big joint decision, after choosing marriage and buying our house. As with those two major decisions, we both just know. I am beginning to recognize that agreement on the big things comes easy for us. This choice will affect and unite us for many years to come. Our mutual commitment to another being seems to affirm our commitment to each other.

What a privileged experience to share. As in being with young children, basking in the presence of the pups allows us to touch those exuberant, yet gentle, places in ourselves.

Our pup is only five-and-one-half weeks old. We can't take her yet. I know from reading in a book I bought about Labrador retrievers that seven-and-one-half to eight weeks

is the ideal time to take them from their litter. This socialization time with her litter is crucial to her development. But
it's torture to leave her for two weeks.

We prepare like parents awaiting the arrival of a newborn.
Petsmart loves us. How about this pink collar? Oh, and a
matching leash, of course. Toys, dish, dog pen and food lay in
place, awaiting her arrival. Our preparation and anticipation
aligns us. Our pup is the first being we are going to nurture
and raise together.

   We toss names around, as expectant parents do. The boys
pitch in. We narrow it down to "Magic" or "Indigo." "Magic"
wins. It is appropriate, as she feels like magic coming into
our lives. She is registered with the American Kennel Club as
"Desperado's Magic of Pineridge" (the name of our street). We
lovingly dub her "Maggie."

   The love between Tom and I is still fresh and exciting, as
is anticipating a new puppy in our home. As when children
come into young relationships, ours is about to change. We
will learn to work together for what's best for this new little
creature that will be totally dependent on us. Like a child,
Maggie will soon reveal our different ways of approaching
things. She will make us see things in ourselves and each
other we may not otherwise learn.

The big day comes at last. "She'll cry the first night," Joan
warns. "Just ignore her. She has to get used to being alone, and
if you go to her, it will take longer to break her of whining."

   We don't know any better. We trust Joan since she has a lot
of experience with puppies and we don't.

   Tom drives home. I cuddle our new bundle. Lucky me.
Intermittent whimpers are muffled as she nestles into my
neck and chest.

"You must be so frightened without your littermates, baby," I tell her softly. I hold her so close. I open my heart wide and she crawls in—an opening that continues to grow for the rest of our lives together. She is already awakening a depth of love in me that had gone underground. That love, passion, and enthusiasm natural to us as young children that can get dampened during socialization by often well-meaning parents, teachers, and even peers. I learned it wasn't safe to express my thoughts, actions, or feelings in my family without the risk of being chastised for not matching some external rule or expectation. I heard too many times in a condescending tone, "You have no common sense!" after spontaneous actions on my part. I shut down. Not that the exuberance, spontaneity, and honesty of children don't sometimes need to be tempered by adults; but when it's done often and in a harsh manner, children lock up beautiful parts of themselves behind doors that will only open again when who they are will be received.

When we arrive home, our new bundle pokes her nose into every nook and cranny. We track her every move, delighting in the brightness emanating from her. Brown eyes glisten. Tail wags her baby-elephant-shaped body. Even now, her exuberance precedes her.

"What is *this* doing here?" Shanna's dilated eyes and indignant look seem to say. Our feline sulks away in disgust.

Maggie's first bounce toward her meets with a hiss and a swat. Our coal black newcomer is a quick study, though. From this point on, she ventures with caution toward our orange and white feline ruler of the roost.

Night falls and bedtime approaches. Following the breeder's recommendation, we put Maggie in her small pen in my office upstairs—alone. She whines as predicted for a long time. It breaks my heart to ignore her. Thinking we are doing the right thing, we let her cry. My gut disagrees with this approach. I ignore it. The breeders are experts with puppies compared to us, right?

A few weeks pass. My sister tells me during a telephone conversation that Heather or Brad slept next to their Brittany spaniel when she was a puppy and comforted her when she whimpered. *Hmm.* Maybe my gut knew better than the breeders did. Although Maggie's crying did lessen and stop after just a few nights.

With a little research, I learn from the Humane Society of Boulder Valley that dogs, like wolves, are pack animals. Their humans are part of their pack. Sleeping in the same den is simply part of pack behavior. Being alone has never been a natural situation for their ancestors, the wolves. Without the connection with her familiar littermates, Maggie must have been terrified. Had we known to let Maggie sleep in a small crate in our room, we would have helped create a sense of security for her, like a crib offers to a baby.

What I'd give to relive these first nights: to lie close to her; offer comfort and warmth; to at least have her kennel in our bedroom. How much more humane it would have been to ease her into short periods of being alone in new surroundings—to help build trust that we would come back.

This is the first time in her life I follow the advice of an expert over my instincts and later regret it. It won't be the last.

Chapter Two
Early Escapades

*H*opefully we are making up for our nighttime mistakes by how much we all dote on Maggie. Tom Jr. is home for Christmas break and cuddles and plays with her. Scott follows her around, giggles, and calls her "Po Po," one of numerous nicknames Maggie collects. On Christmas, Jeff can't keep his hands off of her. He dubs her "Magster," which eventually becomes "Magster-Wagster." I can see why the name "Maggie" elicits a "Margaret" out of Tom and me occasionally. But I have no idea where "J. Margaret Stersley" comes from. Ask any dog guardian. Most of them have numerous names for their dog and often very goofy ones.

Early training based on trust is so critical to a strong relationship with a dog. It is our job as responsible guardians to set up training and the environment for Maggie to succeed. For example, we keep shoes, socks, and other personal items out of her reach and give her toys to chew on. This way she learns fast what is hers to chew and what isn't. At eight weeks old, Maggie's attention span is short. So she and I practice basic commands twice daily in brief ten-minute sessions.

"Maggie, *sit*." Glistening eyes focus on me. I help her behind down gently.

I pat her head and smile at her.

Do I think to wait until she sits on her own and praise her with "Good sit," so she can begin to associate her behavior with the word *sit*? Of course not. Whoops.

"*Stay*." I back away; my palm is out and facing her. What an eager face! Anticipating.

"That's it," I say slowly, so as not to break her concentration.

"Maggie, *come*!" I slap my hands on my thighs to encourage her. She can't get to me fast enough. Pleasing me is her self-appointed job.

"Good girl," I praise. Prance. Wiggle. Wag. She anticipates my next command.

"*Down*." It is clear she enjoys the mental stimulation and wants to please me.

"Yes!" I reach down and rub her.

Maggie increases the behaviors I ask for when I praise her. If my voice reflects irritation or disapproval, her face falls and she keeps her distance. Maggie loves to learn, as long as it is fun and I reward her for correct responses with praise and pets. A reward can be anything a dog enjoys such as a treat, tennis ball, or toy. Maggie is teaching me about positive reinforcement training before I technically know what it is. Reward desired behaviors and they increase. Ignore undesired behaviors and they tend to disappear.[1]

Our training sessions strengthen our growing bond and Maggie's self-confidence. They also establish leadership for her, which every dog needs lest they take it on themselves. As distant relatives of wolves, dogs have similar pack instincts. That includes a social structure with an alpha leader. Without leadership, puppies can turn into uncontrollable dogs with behavior problems or even aggression.[2] These are the dogs that are labeled unmanageable and often end up in shelters.

I wish we knew to offer her more. We only skim the surface of her capabilities. For example, we only teach Maggie a very basic "Come," because that is all we know to do. Do we slowly increase the distance using a long lead? Increase the level of distraction and reward at the same time? No. Why? Because we never look beyond doggie kindergarten.

I later learn that dogs with difficult behavior issues can often be helped by a committed guardian and a competent trainer using reward-based obedience training. I believe we owe our dogs that chance to lay the foundation for a long and happy relationship.

My bond with Maggie is not the only bond that is growing. Tom and I team up to clean her kennel, house-train, play with, and exercise her. As with raising children, caring for our puppy directs our efforts toward a common goal. Like a baby or small child, she is dependent on us. Our combined efforts allow this little being to live and develop. We nurture her life every day and influence who she becomes through our interactions with her. What we give to Maggie and the trials and joy she gives back to us are shared experiences we thrive on. As with children, we share life together in the intimacy of our home and create history together. As a couple, Tom and I are like two legs of a triangle. Maggie is providing the stability of that third leg.

One day, Tom and I both arrive home from work at the same time. Maggie is not yet sixteen weeks old. The stench hits our nostrils as soon as we walk up the stairs into the living room. Our precious black blob bounces ecstatically at our return and pays no heed to where her paws land in her messy pen. Tom and I take a deep sigh, exhausted both from a hard day at work and from the daily kennel duty.

We are silent, frustrated after so many similar cleanup experiences. Tom looks from Maggie to me, and his face melts. Out of the blue, he blurts, "She's just a baby!"

We crack up. This line sticks. We call on it long past puppyhood to lighten us up and buy her a reprieve. Tom cleans her up while I do kennel duty.

For the most part, house-training is a breeze for Maggie, in spite of us. She creates her own separate soiling spot in her large pen and teaches us that she naturally doesn't want to soil her own space. No dog does. We learn that puppies don't have adequate bladder and bowel-muscle control until they are four to five months old. After that time, their ability to hold it gradually increases. The average puppy can hold it for the number of hours that equal how many months old she is plus one, up to a maximum of eight hours.[3]

Do we use a crate to aid in her house training? Well, no. Training information is available at our local humane societies and in books. But like so many busy dog owners, we often fly by the seat of our pants and hope something will magically stick.

As happens so often with kids, the novelty of a new dog wears off. Tom Jr. is back in Greeley at the University of Northern Colorado. That is his life now. Jeff showers Maggie with hugs and kisses when he sees her, but he lives with his mother forty-five minutes away. He is a junior in high school, and peer activities are his top priority. We often meet him in town for dinner, or Tom meets him on his way home from work. Jeff's visits to our home become more sporadic. Scott spends his days trying to ditch as many school days as possible without getting kicked out. Sometimes he exceeds his quota. It takes four schools and two years to complete his senior year in high school. He spends his evenings working (or so we think), dating, or drinking with the guys. For all three boys, Maggie is now an afterthought.

I have a psychotherapy practice in Boulder and have been seeing private clients for five years. I became more interested in alternative healthcare and left my traditional nursing role. I want to make a difference in people's lives in a way that touches their spirit, to help them become more of what they want to be. To help them set themselves free. But burnout is slowly creeping in. I'm beginning to realize I need a more in-depth mental health background than I have to deal effectively with some of the problems my clients are bringing to me, like borderline personality disorder. My own tendency toward perfectionism doesn't help. I expect a lot of myself, and that significantly contributes to my own level of stress.

Maggie is growing. Her baby elephantine body is shifting into that of a sleeker adolescent dog. We leave her in our small kitchen now, with a baby gate, when we leave for work. Upon my return home, I walk up the stairs from the garage. I hear her paws strike the floor after each leap in the air, and her tail thumps its passionate drumbeat wildly against the cabinets. I come into her view in the dining room, her ears go back, and her face softens. She paws the air and seems to say, "Hurry please! I can't wait one more moment to plant my tongue all over your face!" Her greeting nurtures me. It is so pure and simple and such a contrast compared with the complex situations I left behind at my office. My heart overflows. I no longer feel disconnected and alone.

Maggie retrieves balls and Frisbees with gusto. In fact, obsession is a more appropriate term.

"*Drop*, Maggie," I command. Down comes the ball at my feet. "Good girl!"

Hmm. How does she know to do this? She hasn't learned this word or action yet. This response can be conditioned with training, by exchanging the retrieved toy for a treat. I didn't do that. For most things, she requires minimal training. Maggie often seems to understand what I ask of her before I teach her the word.

Yet it's not simple to know the best way to handle behaviors Maggie engages in during her first two years that feel out of my control. Spring blossoms colorful and green when Maggie decides on a little secret escapade out of the yard. I call repeatedly for her from the front and back doors. I search our street on foot. Finally, I aim my car toward the beach area. There she is, trotting and sniffing up the street with her tail pointing at the sky, exploring her way back home. She is soaking wet after her clandestine journey to the lake for a swim. Her face lights up when she sees me, delighted and surprised to meet up with Mom.

Mom, however, is not too happy with this little prank. She bounces toward me with her distinctive "Maggie-smile." But in my fear, I yell at her for being in the street. This is another moment I'd give anything to live over again. Her countenance collapses. She sits with her ears back and paws the air. Her face pleads, "*Please* don't be mad at me. I didn't mean it. Just love me, okay?"

I feel so guilty for having scolded her. I realize after the fact that I unintentionally had her associate coming to me with being scolded—bad timing. It was actually too late to reprimand her by the time I caught up with Maggie. Her mistake was in the past. I had set her up to fail by leaving her outside unattended for too long. Perhaps I am the one who needs the most training.

Weeks later, I bake a special sugarless apple pie for Tom and leave it on the stove to cool. I am upstairs in my office when Maggie appears. She looks sheepish.

"Hi, baby love," I welcome her. "What's that on your face? Why do you look like you're in trouble?"

Suddenly, I know. But how did *she* know to be guilty? Our girl loves to eat. I remember the pie. Plastered on her snout are remnants of my labor of love. I dash downstairs. The plate is upside-down on the floor. I cringe as I turn it over. Empty.

A few mashed apples dot the floor and are all that remain. I choke back tears. In my ignorance, I spank her. This is the second and last time I inappropriately blame Maggie for something that is poor management on my part. Taking my frustration out on her, especially after the fact, only serves to damage her trust in me. Again, the lesson is mine. Don't leave food on the counter within paw's reach. Lucky for me, her unconditional love for me forgives my leadership errors.

I learn with Maggie just how much I *don't* know about dogs. For example, with leash walking, Maggie is a real puller. This makes for a wrestling match for us on the other end of her leash, and excessive pressure on her throat. The more I pull back on her leash against her collar, the harder she lunges forward. What Maggie is showing me just doesn't click: that dogs have a reflex to actually pull in the opposite direction from the pull they feel against their collar. The pressure not only stresses her throat, but is also hard on the neck vertebrae and discs.

"Why don't you try a Haltie?" Tom's sister, Lou, had trained dogs at the Humane Society in Denver as a volunteer and suggests this to us.

We try it. It acts much like a halter on a horse. It guides her head around quite gently when she pulls. But Maggie tosses her head and rubs it on the ground, paws at the Haltie, and tries to get it off. I think we're being cruel. It seems more like a muzzle to me, a restriction on her mouth. I refuse to use it. I don't realize I simply need to desensitize Maggie to the Haltie or Gentle Leader on her face. We could have done that by treating and praising her when we initially put it on her, then removing it immediately. By keeping it on a little longer each time over a few days, continuing the praise and treat routine, Maggie would have adjusted to it.[4] Using a Gentle Leader or a Haltie is a much kinder choice for teaching a dog not to pull. A chest harness is another option. And with appropriate training, most dogs can eventually learn to walk with a loose leash. But I don't learn any of this until much later from positive reinforcement training books. So our leash struggle continues.

Training has its limits when my high-spirited girl makes up her mind to act on an irresistible temptation. In June, spring runoff is at its peak in the Rocky Mountains when we hike the Sourdough Trail in the Indian Peaks Wilderness. Tom rides the same route on his mountain bike. Rugged peaks kiss a deep blue sky punctuated with cotton-ball clouds. The rushing St. Vrain River thunders closer. Maggie is not on her leash. I am focused on the wildflower medley along the trail. My eyes drift lazily back to her. Her ears perk up and her body twitches. But I see her body language too late, then make the mistake of trusting her to heed my call. Her instinctual love of the water calls louder. She dashes ahead toward the roaring river.

"Maggie, come! Maggie, no!" My screams fade behind her. I race after her while my heart pounds. The river comes into view. I watch, horrified, as Maggie bolts into the roaring turbulence. She is swept downstream in seconds, while I stand alone and helpless on the bank.

"Maggie, come!" As though she can. Foolish me. From a distance, she looks over her shoulder with a baffled expression before she disappears around the bend. In a panic, I tear through bushes and make my way downstream. I struggle through and around thick brush. No sign of Maggie. My heart is in my throat. Tears well in my eyes. After what seems a lifetime, Maggie maneuvers out of the rapids into an eddy. I finally reach her and throw my arms around her. I hold her tight and close.

"Oh Maggie, thank God you're okay! Please don't ever do that again!"

Even she is shaking.

I think Maggie read the fear in my voice that day. This is the last time she ignores my command on our many hikes near rushing streams and rivers.

I have no idea how to train our curious adventurer to stay in our unfenced yard. I walk the perimeter of our wooded acre and point out to Miss Magster her invisible boundaries. Having had two dogs hit by cars as a child, it is crucial to me that she not venture into the street off-leash. I point to the road. "This is no." This is *not* the way to do boundary training, I learn later. Yet she stays within these boundaries. She somehow understands what I want; but *how*? Does she tune into my *vision* of her staying in our yard? Or dropping the Frisbee and ball?

Contrary to the old adage "you can't teach an old dog new tricks," Maggie demonstrates ongoing learning as the years march on. There's nothing like the ease with which the canine-human relationship flows once your dog is integrated into your family. She is house-trained. Loyal. She wants to please and is responsive to your commands; what once took heaps of time and energy now flows like warm honey. Your many efforts are rewarded.

With Maggie, what seems a magical anticipation or mind-reading of my wishes continues to grow. Her level of presence opens my heart—a presence I share with no human in this way. I have found a soul companion.

Chapter Three
Beyond Words: Scent or Telepathy?

*I*t's April again and we drive the twenty-two hours to South Padre Island—a funky little spit of land at the tip of Texas between the Laguna Madre and the Gulf of Mexico—for our annual group windsurfing trip. It's Maggie's first long road trip with us.

What a delight to watch Maggie bursting at the seams at her first sight of the ocean. She is in heaven. She plunges in and out of the Gulf waves, face bright and alive, and fetches the tennis ball repeatedly. Then she bolts full speed up and down the sandy beach—deliriously happy. Smiles appear on the faces of many beach walkers. Following her ocean romp, I reach for her collar to place her leash on. But her unbridled enthusiasm is a step ahead of me. She spots a small boy. Before I can catch her, Maggie plants her paws on his small shoulders. He loses his balance and lands on his back in the sand with Maggie joyfully licking his face. Tom and I are mortified. I apologize profusely. Lucky for us, his father takes it well, and the bewildered child breaks into a smile instead of bawling.

I put the leash on. Rather than me walking her, however, Maggie has a different idea. She grabs the leash in her mouth and runs sideways and backward down the beach, with occasional leaps into the air. Her whole being seems to say, "Come on! Let's make leash walking fun, not boring!" Her practice of dancing home in like manner following regular swims in our neighborhood lake resumes upon our return, which comes sooner than expected.

Our house sitter calls. It's Shanna. She is very ill and at a veterinary clinic. She is too weak to stand or support her head. It's a form of kidney disease. Her kidneys are dumping too much potassium.

We fear the worst. But when we finally get to the clinic after two days of driving, she purrs the moment she sees us.

"She should be fine with this potassium supplement," her vet informs us. I am thrilled to be taking her home, because I thought this was the end. I'm impressed with these vets who brought Shanna back from the brink of death. But her comeback is slow.

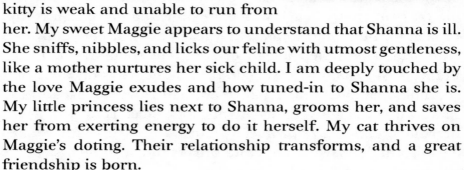

Up to this point, Shanna kept her distance from Maggie. But now my kitty is weak and unable to run from her. My sweet Maggie appears to understand that Shanna is ill. She sniffs, nibbles, and licks our feline with utmost gentleness, like a mother nurtures her sick child. I am deeply touched by the love Maggie exudes and how tuned-in to Shanna she is. My little princess lies next to Shanna, grooms her, and saves her from exerting energy to do it herself. My cat thrives on Maggie's doting. Their relationship transforms, and a great friendship is born.

"She's not just your run-of-the-mill Lab," Tom offers. "There's more to her. She's got the whole package. She's a lover of people *and* other animals. She's playful, exuberant, and so devoted to us, including the cat. She's just a hell of a dog."

After Shanna recovers, Maggie pokes and nibbles her into

play and then jumps back from her quick-moving claws. The two new friends frolic daily with each other for nearly two years. They are often side-by-side outdoors, so I never worry about a fox or coyote grabbing Shanna.

In February 1993, we lose Shanna just before her sixteenth birthday. What an empty space she leaves in our home and hearts. Maggie mourns her as much as we do. When we leave her home alone now, there is a new look on her face—sadness. She misses her buddy.

Three months pass. We aren't ready for another cat. But Maggie is. Our neighbor, Madonna, is fostering a litter of kittens in her home for the local humane society. We choose the one that prances over, swats Madonna's Saint Bernard, Bud, on the paw, and runs. And so it is that one spicy little ball of fire comes home to be Maggie's kitty. It is love at first sight for both of them.

Maggie dotes upon Cinnamon—who is no bigger than the palm of mpy hand—as though she is her own puppy. It's not unusual to find Maggie's front legs up on our bed, wrapped around our kitten as they both sleep.

Maggie is clearly Cinnamon's main connection. Our little orange Siamese-Tabby mix seldom finds her way into our bed, but sleeps cuddled against her best buddy. Once again, Maggie has a little pal to protect outdoors. They often explore side-by-side amidst the scrub oak and pine trees, a déjà vu of Maggie and Shanna.

As Cinnamon grows, she decides it's her job to groom our

shiny seventy-two-pound black canine. Each day, Maggie tolerates cat claws hooked into her jowls while Cinnamon ceremoniously bathes eyelids, inner ears, and eventually her entire head with purpose. Maggie returns the favor and nibbles Cinnamon's entire body.

In time, Maggie's motherly guarding, licking, and cuddling gives way to nudging and nosing our little orange dart into play. Maggie stalks Cinnamon, and then dashes in front of her, enticing our cat with play bows. Quick moves to dodge the claws follow. Then Cinnamon struts coyly by our willing Lab with that "come-and-get-me" look. She seems to signal, "Let's play, Mags!" And play they do, for many happy years.

Our mischievous fluffy feline ignores her scratch posts and creates her own out of our dining room chairs. This is becoming a daily ritual, and I'm not pleased.

"Cinnamon, no! Stop clawing the chairs!" I yell. Then a curious thing happens. Maggie decides to help me out. The moment she sees or hears Cinnamon clawing the chairs, Maggie springs toward her and nips her in good-natured fashion. She succeeds in chasing Cinnamon away from the chairs. My sensitive best friend knows exactly what I want after she hears me reprimand Cinnamon a few times. Maggie takes the action that the situation demands. She takes over my job to stop Cinnamon from ruining our furniture.

I do talk to Maggie continually, as though I *expect* her to understand and respond to my wishes.

"Excuse me," I say if she is in my way. She moves aside to

let me pass.

When I open her food cabinet, she sticks her head in to search for goodies. Of course, I can't get my hands into it with half of her body inside of it.

"Back up, Mags." Backward she steps.

Maggie loves to park in the middle of our tiny kitchen floor. She likes being close to the food source. But it makes cooking space a bit too cozy and tight.

"Move, Maggie." She gets up, sulks into the dining room, and positions herself where she can keep her eye on me.

Not until I stop and realize what she is doing does her level of responsiveness begin to awaken me to a bigger picture. It's known that dogs can be trained to understand and respond to many words. But I didn't teach Maggie these words. What can explain this? I begin to wonder if animals rise to the occasion and respond according to the potential their guardians see in them, just as humans tend to perform according to what's expected of them. Through Maggie, I am learning that if I respectfully expect her to be intelligent and understand what I want, she will respond to that expectation. Is that true of all dogs?

I am the student here, realizing that many humans, including myself, may have underestimated what animals are capable of figuring out and tuning in to. A sixteen-month-old toddler may not be developmentally capable of saying the word *shoe* yet, but he will point to his foot when you ask him where his shoes are. He knows exactly what you mean. Is it possible that our dogs and other animals understand our words or the gist of our conversations, but we think they don't simply because they can't speak? The more I see Maggie as an intelligent, emotional being, and the deeper our bond becomes, the more she seems to manifest these qualities.

When I dress for work, Maggie examines my skirt or slacks by flipping them up with her nose. She sulks away in disgust, flops onto the bedroom carpet with a great sigh, and rests her head on her paws. She avoids my eyes except for an occasional raised eyebrow. There she lay, even as I walk out the door, in obvious disappointment. My casual clothes evoke a very different response. After one sniff, the tail starts its swing. She pushes her nose deeper into my clothes as though drinking in the scent of us hanging out and playing together. My black beauty queen prances, her eyes twinkle, and she exudes excitement. Of course, her nose informs her of my plans.

But an amazing thing happens when I have a short workday. I stand in the bathroom in my dress clothes and apply my makeup. I *consider* the pros and cons of taking Maggie and letting her wait for me in the car. Without my saying a word, she appears and looks up at me with expectant, hopeful eyes that say, "Can I? Can I please?"

Her relentless stare bores straight into my heart. If I'm leaning toward leaving her home but am still wavering, she follows me down the stairs to the front door. She senses my incongruence and uses it to sway me. Her imploring expression is impossible to resist. Maggie usually wins.

On warm days, I take Maggie swimming. During cooler weather, we often hike together. The time we leave varies from day to day. When I merely start *thinking* about leaving for the lake or the trail, up she jumps from her nap and trots into the room I'm in. Ears perk up. Her expectant expression says, "Let's go. I'm ready!"

How does Maggie know when I am planning to leave even before I engage in getting-ready behaviors? This is far from an occasional occurrence. She demonstrates an apparent awareness of my intentions on a regular basis. I didn't know this was possible. I can't attribute it to training or habit. I don't know how to explain our communication. We are on the same wavelength, but how?

J. Allen Boone speaks of a similar experience with

Strongheart, the famous Hollywood dog who played leading roles in the movies *The Silent Call, Brawn of the North, The Love Master,* and Jack London's *White Fang.* Mr. Boone cared for Strongheart in his home when Strongheart's owner was temporarily called away from California. One day, he sat at his typewriter wondering if he should finish his writing job or take Strongheart for a walk in the hills for the day. He decided on the walk. He states, "Within a few seconds after this decision had been made, the back door was knocked violently open and in rushed Strongheart in a frenzy of excitement. Skidding to where I was sitting, he gave the back of one of my hands a brief dab with his tongue, raced into the bedroom, and came out almost immediately with the old sweater I always wore on our outings. Then into the bedroom again and back with my blue jeans. Then came one of my walking boots. Then its mate. Then my Irish walking stick. All of these things he carefully placed at my feet ... How did the dog know that I had changed my plans and was going to take him on an outing? There had been no outward communication between us at all ... In the supposed privacy of my own mind, I had suddenly changed intention, and then he appeared on the scene knowing all about it."[1]

Just as Strongheart appeared to read Mr. Boone's thoughts, Maggie seems to know my intentions and wishes. We landscape our front walkway. I just finish planting flower terraces bordering both sides of the new flagstone steps. Up until now, Maggie has spent years cutting across what had been weeds to get up the small hill into the yard. Now this is my flower garden. How am I ever going to keep her out of my flowers? Three narrow stairs between the planter and the terraces lead up to the yard.

I walk down the main steps with Maggie on my heels. I point to my tender new flowers on each side and say, "These are Mom's flowers, baby girl. You need to stay out of them."

I lead her to the narrow rock steps and point. "This is where you can go, Mags." She follows me up the steps. "Good girl." It takes only one demonstration.

The hose spool blocks Maggie's easy passage from the porch to the steps when I water my flowers. She sits on the porch patiently and watches me until I move the spool or she gingerly steps around it. Her paws land on flagstone, not dirt. Maggie honors my wish and my love of my flowers; she *never* steps in them. Is it the enormous amount of time we spend together—more time than I spend with any human—that allows her inherent ability to read me to grow through the years?

There are reports of epileptics whose dogs alert them to an impending seizure. One theory is that these dogs can smell the chemical changes that occur in their guardians' brains prior to the seizure. Do chemical changes occur in my body with each different thought and emotion that Maggie can smell? The field of psychoneuroimmunology has demonstrated that our thoughts create chemicals in our bodies.[2] Perhaps through their incredible sense of smell, our canine companions can detect our thoughts and intentions at a sophisticated level that we have not considered before.

Likewise, the *Santa Maria Times* reported on a woman (Jill Meza) with diabetes and a heart arrhythmia. Her dog, Cinnamon, consistently alerted her prior to drops in blood sugar and her irregular heart rhythm by whining and pacing anxiously, unable to be consoled. The dog was later trained more specifically to push on Jill's left leg prior to the occurrence of her heart problem and on her right leg if her blood sugar was getting too low. When Jill was on a trip to Cuba without her dog, she *dreamed* that Cinnamon was pushing persistently on her right leg and then going to sit by the refrigerator. Jill got up and checked her blood sugar, and it was dangerously low. Upon Jill's return, the friend that kept Cinnamon reported that the dog did fine except for Tuesday night, when she became very agitated and woke everyone up in the house. They were unable to comfort her. Cinnamon's agitation coincided with Jill's hypoglycemia attack in Cuba![3] Scent can't account for her dog's alerting behavior in this case. There seems to be an extrasensory telepathic connection at work here.

These invisible, unexplainable connections fascinate me, as do dreams. My intrigue with dreams began when I was in my twenties, after my grandmother (Nanny) died. We'd had a very close relationship. I didn't get back to Indiana in time to say good-bye, so I remained unsettled and incomplete because I didn't have closure with her. Four months later, Nanny appeared to me in radiance in a dream—although it seemed more like a vision than any dream I'd ever had. We expressed our love for each other and said our good-byes—without uttering a word—telepathically. My unrest and regret faded into peaceful acceptance after that.

Now I keep a dream journal. I pen them as soon as I wake up, or whatever fragments I remember. The more I record, the more I remember. Although I am disillusioned with organized religion, spirituality is still a vital force in my life. I have come to believe dreams are communications from our souls, our individual pipelines to divine intelligence, like guiding beacons that point to personal lessons we need to learn and grow from.

According to Jungian dream analysis, the soul is thought to have the ability to transcend the physical world and travel in the realm of the collective unconscious in our dreams. The collective unconscious is where we come from, we return to it when we can, and we ultimately return to it when we die. Dreams are an exceptional source of information, inspiration, and enlightenment that can lead to a fuller life. As you attempt to comprehend their messages, you may gain insight into your daily life and into your soul. "The unconscious mind may have the power to connect us to other levels, or dimensions, of ourselves and eventually to everyone and everything else, including Divinity."[4]

Most religions believe that humans are all connected spiritually. Native Americans extend that belief to all living things. Can *any* being communicate with us spirit-to-spirit through our dreams? Even our dogs, as Jill's did?

Does an energetic link exist between Maggie's soul and mine, between Jill and her dog Cinnamon—born out of the deep love and spiritual bond between us—that allows for communication to pass between us telepathically? The communication that occurs between Maggie and me and the others mentioned above can't be explained by the sensory world. If anyone had told me before my relationship with Maggie that animals have the potential for telepathic communication, I would have laughed. Not anymore. I now suspect our deep bonds with our animals foster telepathy between us.

Why do some dogs exhibit alerting abilities while others, like Maggie and Strongheart, appear to read our thoughts? Certain Eastern religions believe that some humans are advanced souls. Might the same be true of dogs and other animals?

Chapter Four
Dogs Don't Get DUIs

*A*s I notice how tuned-in Maggie is to me, Scott is becoming more tuned-out with Tom and me. He is between high schools once again and still has not graduated. I initially feel tremendous compassion for Scott's difficulties, since I know he and Tom Jr. witnessed domestic abuse by their stepfather against their mother. In addition, they had been neglected at times when their mother and stepfather were drunk. They were actually left behind in restaurants.

"You abandoned us!" Scott screams at Tom one night down in the family room during one of their frequent arguments.

"When? No, I didn't!" Tom yells back. "I lived a mile away, and you were with me four nights a week!" he implores Scott to realize. At this, Maggie gets up from her snooze and heads upstairs. The tension is too much for her. I soon follow, initially confused at Scott's accusation.

I sit down on the steps going up to my office. Maggie saunters out of our bedroom, sits on the step above me in her unique way, and rests her head on top of mine. It feels protective, like she is comforting me.

I can see both of Tom and Scott's perspectives after thinking about it. They are both right. Scott felt abandoned by his father in that he had to deal alone with neglect and domestic violence. Perhaps he felt his dad should have protected him and he didn't. Tom, on the other hand, thought he was as close and available to his children as possible in the days when the courts strongly favored the mother having custody unless gross neglect or abuse could be proven.

Unknown to Tom, Tom Jr. and Scott lived under the threat from their stepfather that he would harm Tom if either of the boys whispered a word regarding their own neglect or the abuse to their mother. So they remained silent for years out of fear, until Tom Jr. finally spilled the beans. That was it. Tom went to Sharon, his ex-wife, and told her the boys were not coming back. She would have to take him to court to fight it. She never did. His boys remained with him from the ages of ten and twelve.

I understand how those terrible wounds impacted both boys deeply. Scott impresses me as quite sensitive. He and I discuss counseling to help him work through and heal these issues. He says he wants to go. So I set up an appointment for him, with his permission. He doesn't show up. He has an excuse. I buy it. He assures me again he really wants to see a counselor. I arrange a second appointment. He blows it off. He has another excuse.

"It isn't my fault," Scott defends with intensity.

I never try again.

Scott blames his family history for his poor school and work performance. I am beginning to see that rather than take responsibility to heal his emotional pain, he wants his family to feel sorry for him. He seems to use his past to induce guilt and pity to get what he wants. I watch him incessantly try to manipulate Tom for money. He attempts it with me, too.

I begin to see that Scott gets more out of getting people to take care of him than finding his self-esteem by supporting and caring for himself. My trust in Scott's sincerity lessens. Although I continue to have compassion for his history, I begin to realize he isn't ready or willing to deal with it. He seems more interested in *using* his past to blame others and to not follow through. I don't quite understand or respect that he turns away from solutions and seems to prefer being a victim.

A young woman at the alternative high school Scott attended files a restraining order against him. She calls to tell Tom and me very apologetically how much she didn't want to do it but felt no other recourse since Scott won't leave her alone. According to Scott, he did nothing. This is part of the difficulty for Tom and me. In Scott's eyes, he is completely innocent. Nothing is *ever* his responsibility.

He quits another job and begins parking in front of the television on the couch during the day. This violates a boundary we set that if he isn't in school, he has to have a job to keep living here. Scott is smart. He knows how invested Tom is in his graduating. I don't think he believes Tom will follow through on this rule, so he pushes the limits. It begins to dawn on Tom that he has to let go of his emotional investment in Scott completing high school, or Scott will orchestrate the tune and Tom will keep dancing to it.

I feel like the door I tried to open out of compassion, understanding, and a hope for healing Scott slammed shut. His is a dance I don't wish to follow.

Yet I don't fully trust my perception of Scott. I second-guess myself. His attitude of innocence is compelling. And after all, he did experience another major emotional blow with Tom's divorce from his stepmother. That could be enough to create the issues we're dealing with, right? And he experienced trauma in his childhood....

He gets a job with Nissan Auto in town. I become suspicious when he doesn't always leave the house at a time congruent with the time he is supposed to be at work. I share my suspicions with Tom, but he thinks I'm wrong. He so wants to believe that Scott is at work. I finally phone Nissan one evening only to learn that Scott stopped going to work a month earlier. What had he been doing?

"No, he wasn't fired," the woman informs me. "He had a job. He just quit coming."

We are perplexed. Tom is really upset. We don't appreciate being lied to. We suspected lies before with some of Scott's stories, but here there is no question. This is the last straw for us. I walk over and put my arms around Tom. Maggie must sense our resignation, for she walks over, licks and nibbles our chins, going from one to the other. She loves it when we are at her level. I'm struck with how the ease of caring for our furry children stands out in stark contrast to the difficulty that interacting with Scott poses.

Naturally, in Scott's eyes, Nissan wronged him, so he quit. But he didn't bother to inform them—or us. We tell Scott to move out. Happening this way makes it more painful for Tom.

With Scott gone, Tom and I begin to experience a calmer home without steady drama and tension. It's amazing how readily our animals took a backseat through the trials with Scott and how quickly they come to the forefront now that there is room.

Rather than get a job to support himself, Scott chooses to move back in with his mother. It isn't long before he lands his first DUI. But he isn't alone for long. Jeff and Tom Jr. soon follow suit.

The more difficulties we encounter with the boys, the more I recognize how easy raising Maggie is compared to parenting a child. What a treasure she is. In spite of our mistakes, Maggie gives us her unconditional love and trust. I wonder how Tom sees it. I have my chance to ask him on a late-summer mountain hike to Blue Lake in the Indian Peaks Wilderness. Maggie runs ahead through a meadow of lavender asters. The wildflower explosion we found there in mid-July is past its peak, but it is still lush and exhilarating. Streams still run, the peaks crest in their glory, and as always, the high alpine setting feeds my soul.

"Having a dog like Maggie is real similar to a relationship with *young* children in that when you come home, you're greeted by children or a dog in much the same way," Tom says. "If they're not distracted, there's nothing else that matters to them. You're greeted totally. And it's a pleasure to watch both young children and dogs develop."

"It truly is a joy to observe children and pups learn and discover their world, isn't it?" I agree.

"Absolutely. As is playing with them. When I play ball with Maggie or take her for a hike, it just warms my heart to see her pleasure," Tom shares. "Like that. There she goes again," he points.

The snow field comes into view, with a patch of black sliding down it, feet kicking wildly into the air. Her hind end sticks up in a play bow, and then she does a face plant, followed by that big dog smile of hers.

"Where were we? I get so lost in the moment with her that I forget what we're saying. I wanted to ask you something. Oh, right. What differences do you see between having Maggie in our lives compared with raising your children?"

"There is quite a difference between pets and children in the degree of demands placed on parents. When kids are little, you're already saving money for college. It requires so much to raise kids. With dogs, you don't have to deal with the influence of society like you do kids. A dog doesn't care what brand name the collar around her neck is. Our kids are taught by our consumer-oriented society and television commercials that they should have a certain brand name. 'All the other kids have it. I should too.' Kids are programmed and feel entitled to it. When you have kids—one or two or three more consuming bodies—what it takes from the parents is huge. Dogs want good food, nice tennis balls, and affection. The basics. Like little kids before they get so swayed by society—a sway that starts as soon as they go to school."

"I've never had to deal with Maggie getting a DUI, but I dealt with *all* my boys having DUIs. I never had to deal with a dog openly defying me about something where I had to be the real heavy. With a dog, their upset only goes on for a very short period of time. With my kids, it was like war. It could go on for days if I denied them something."

"That must have been hard on you. Unlike Maggie," I interject. "She just accepts it when we refuse a toy she offers us to play with, and she forgives and trusts us immediately, even if we get mad and reprimand her. With kids, the walls start to come up."

"The walls do come up," Tom agrees. "Kids want what they want; if you don't provide it, the friction starts, and it builds and builds. Dogs live in the present and don't carry grudges. Kids carry grudges. This makes the bond with a dog much simpler. The bonds with children are much more complex. My kids want things from me; they have expectations of me. Scott would love it if I paid his bills every month. Maggie just wants me to feed her and take her to play. It gives me that same kind of connection without the overwhelming demand."

"And if you're at all wishy-washy with kids, they'll make your life miserable," Tom continues. "You have to be firm with your boundaries and limits."

"If you're wishy-washy with a dog, that comes back to haunt you too," I add.

"It does, but there are bigger issues with kids. The issue may not be whether you leave the yard or not. The issue may be drugs."

"The potential for stress is obviously much higher for a parent. Like with Scott, your concern for him finishing school and what that means for him, for his life. And then you wonder how far your responsibility as a parent goes in regards to this?"

"Parenting is a difficult job. It can be very tiring. I'm growing as an individual at the same time my children are growing and developing. I don't have it down, yet I'm trying to raise and influence children who *really* don't have it yet."

"I'm sure the potential to blame your parenting skills for a problem in your child is much greater than the tendency to blame yourself for not knowing certain dog-training techniques. I sure don't feel like  I have this training thing down with Maggie, but the stakes aren't as great or long-lasting when she doesn't come when we call her."

"And she's *still* a great dog," Tom smiles.

We feel lucky to be entrusted with her. And it is a trust—a gift. We can't *own* her any more than we can own a child. Maggie walks over for a drink out of her water bottle.

Tom and I began with a very different perspective of how a dog blends into daily life than what Maggie teaches us little by little. We envisioned Fido sitting in the backyard wagging his tail, waiting for his people to come home. And once in awhile, your dog went places with you, so leaving Maggie home as company for Cinnamon isn't uncommon. This will change over time.

A simple walk in the neighborhood is enough for exercise, right? Wrong. Maggie chases Frisbees and swims after balls for hours. She loves hiking with me. What we observe in her is that she needs at least a good hour of hard exercise each day, as do many sporting breeds.

Maggie is teaching us that having a dog in our life involves a large commitment. She also deserves adequate health care, love, and respect. As responsible guardians, we owe her more than the basics of food, water, and shelter. Daily exercise, play, and training provide her with needed mental stimulation—very different than our Fido image. Most often, it is a pleasure. And of course, at times it's a chore. As with children, consistency is important. Unlike a teenager, though, she is easy to please, and her behavior is more predictable. She cuts us slack if we leave a step out now and then.

Maggie springs ahead into Blue Lake before we reach it. We sit on the rocks, toss a stick into the ice-cold water, and watch her paddle with Mount Toll in the background.

None of us are in any hurry to start back down.

Chapter Five
What Pure Joy She Is

*T*om Jr. is required by the court to attend an alcohol program at Colorado State University (CSU) for his DUI. He invites Tom and me to attend his program graduation day, which entails a ropes course and group discussion. A ropes-course program may challenge individuals both physically and emotionally to confront their fears and anxieties. Groups work together as a team to accomplish a task and overcome obstacles. It's designed to promote trust, cooperation, and leadership. Other outcomes include enhancement of self-confidence, self-esteem, and risk-taking.[1] It opens more doors between Tom Jr. and us, and we can see that he is beginning to recognize a choice point. He can go down the same road his mother did or choose a more life-affirming path. It's great for us to see this light go on for him, but it proves to be only an important first step.

Jeff moves to Summit County to follow his Olympic skiing dream. It doesn't turn out as he'd hoped. He leaves snow behind for good when he follows his mother to Hawaii. It doesn't take Jeff long to fall in love and marry Robin, who we adore. But with living so far away, we don't see much of him.

I don't see Scott often while he is living with his mom. Tom, however, meets him weekly for dinner on his way home from Denver. We receive great news—Scott completed high school. We are thrilled as we watch him walk up to the stage to receive his diploma during his graduation ceremony.

Our pride soon turns to concern, though, when Scott receives *another* DUI. The court orders him to do outpatient alcohol rehabilitation. Scott's car insurance becomes prohibitive—he will spend the next two years on foot until his first DUI comes off his record. At least we can breathe easier during that time, knowing he or someone else is less likely to become a drunk-driver statistic. Tom creates more emotional distance with Scott. He's been through drinking issues with his own father and his ex-wife. He can hardly believe he's dealing with it again, in his son, no less.

With the boys following their own paths now, Maggie becomes even more central to our lives. It's the simple, everyday things that endear her to us. In a way no human can be, Maggie is my best friend.

She is beautiful, bred to be a show dog. We don't care about that. We never intend to show her. She has a thick, wavy coat and is stockier than the thinner hunting Labrador breed.

The pounding of her paw steps as she runs down the hall when she hears my feet hit the floor in the morning welcome me to my day with joy. When I lounge in bed longer than usual, she comes in and drapes herself across my belly and rests her head on her paws. She cloaks me in love until I announce, "Okay, let's get up!" Then she bounces off, grabs her favorite fuzzy dolly, and engages me in a few rounds of fetch before she leads me to the kitchen for her morning treat. Thus begins my day, with a welcome brighter than sunshine. As children do, Maggie brings life to our home.

"Okay, princess, go tell everyone who you are." It's time to go outside and announce herself to the hidden wildlife and the neighbors. I watch her wiggle her boxy head between the slats on the deck railing and let go with her high-pitched *"Woo-woo-woo-woo-woo"* that reminds both Tom and me of Curly on *The Three Stooges.*

After her post-breakfast snooze, Miss Mags is on my heels—glued to me. "Are we going now?" Her hopeful dark eyes question. "Isn't it time?"

Maggie thrives on going places, whether it's for a swim, a hike, to greet people at the coffee shop, or a ride in the car to run errands. She holds her head out of the car window as we drive through Boulder, and her floppy velvet ears flap in the breeze. Her inviting brown eyes drink in and radiate love to all life going by. I watch her in my side mirror and etch her precious open look in my memory. Her beautiful spirit shines through her eyes—it softens and warms me.

The employees at McGuckin's, the local hardware store, know Maggie by name and readily treat her from their supply of doggie delights that fill their vest pockets. When Maggie spots a green-vested person, she scrambles up to him, stares, and wiggles at his feet. Maggie adores Patty, one of the employees who offers her treats with gusto like no other. Maggie leaps ecstatically in the air when Patty approaches in her tantalizing manner. McGuckin's is Maggie's favorite stop, as it is for most Boulder dogs.

In 1994, I go back to school at the University of Colorado Health Sciences Center to obtain a master's degree in a family nurse practitioner program. I want to integrate traditional Western medicine with alternative health practices to offer patients a holistic approach in my practice. I'm not totally congruent with this choice, so it is a struggle for me to put in so much intellectual time and energy into a path I am unsure of. Something else is nagging at me inside, another calling, but I don't know what it is or how to answer it.

Maggie and I sit at the Brewing Market coffee shop, my outdoor "office" for studying. My black beauty queen places herself in the middle of the sidewalk—where people walking to and from McGuckin's next door have to notice her. Each new person, dog, or object is cause for jubilation. People lost inside their problems and worries land in the present moment when Maggie prances in front of them—like they are just who she is there to see—as though she's known them forever. Serious frowns melt into big grins when she leaps with elation at their approach. I swell with pride to see this being I am blessed to share life with light up everyone's day. People transform before my eyes as they step out of their heads and into their hearts. For a brief time, their troubles appear to fade. Stressful, busy days appear temporarily forgotten. Even the dryness of what I am studying has spice added to it with Maggie's heartwarming ability to reach out and bring people into our circle. Little does she know she's contributing to my health since it's been shown that social interactions create healthier people.

One study reports that pet-owning couples have more frequent interactions with other people and with each other than couples without pets.[2] I'm not surprised. Dogs don't follow the same conventions people do. They only know how to be their genuine selves. Maggie saunters straight up to people, invited or not. Her spontaneity and unpredictability often trigger unpretentious conversations between strangers and me, and time and again, she makes us laugh together. More good medicine.

People also approach us. "I need a dog fix. We're here on vacation, and mine is at home."

Or perhaps they recently lost their own dog and dearly miss him. Whether human or canine approaches first, Maggie helps us break through social barriers, which allows for more earnest interactions. Dog guardians meet a lot of people that way. Dogs are in the moment. They help us join them.

"Now *that* is a special dog," a woman on the Mesa trail says tenderly. "You can tell just by looking at her face." I am beaming. She isn't the first.

"She has such a presence about her," she continues. "Soul just pours through her eyes." I meet the woman's eyes and see her own light burning there. Is it just that Maggie's spirit facilitates people to touch the love in their hearts, or is it also that one kindred spirit simply recognizes another when they meet?

There was a time I thought Maggie greeted people simply because she loved the attention that came with it. Although I'm sure she thrives on it, I believe there is more to it. Just as we come into this world to offer our unique gifts, to serve life, perhaps Maggie also has a job to do. She gives her energy and enthusiasm to those who cross her path, seems to make their day, and reminds them to smell the flowers. For a few moments, she appears to connect them to themselves, to life, and to us. Can my own purpose in life that I seem to forever chase after be simply this?

Rare is the time anyone passes her without stopping. And we are the luckiest of all, being graced by her presence in our everyday lives.

Chapter Six
She Is My Rock

*B*y now, Tom and I are well past the honeymoon and into the *work* of our marriage. Our values are very similar, as are our spiritual and political orientations. But communication regarding issues *between* us is another story. We both came from parents in conflicted marriages with very limited communication skills. I watched resentment build between my parents as a result of not talking things through, so I am determined to sweep nothing under the rug. Tom, on the other hand, was so affected by his parents' constant bickering that he is determined to avoid conflicts altogether. You can imagine how we clash in our approaches. I bring up the problems I perceive and not always with finesse. I'm not well received, whether my approach is blunt or tactful. Our arguments become more about the process of *how* we respond to each other in conflict rather than to solve the initial difficulty raised. I often feel accused and misunderstood—as does Tom. Counseling helps. It's not a cure.

Maggie is so sensitive to our voice tones. When we argue, her discomfort is easy to detect, as are most of her wide range of emotions. Through shifts in her eye shape and size and how her ears lay on her head, we can easily read that Maggie hates our quarrelling. She exits the dining room to get away from us. I look for her when Tom and I adequately resolve the issue or let it go for the time being. She covers my face with kisses, senses my hurt. I turn even more to Maggie—always there—and show my vulnerability with her more willingly than I do with any human. There are no walls, no judgments between us. She is my rock.

May rolls around and brings my parents here for their annual visit from Indiana. One night, I stand on the porch waiting for Maggie to do her final duty before bed. My mom watches from the top of the stairs in the hall.

"Why do you go out with her? You know she's not going to run away."

"Bears and mountain lions wander into our neighborhood, Mom."

"And what would you *do* if one attacked her?"

Good question. I believe I would do anything to protect Maggie, as a mother would risk her own life for her child. I don't think I would think twice. It's instinct, even if it's stupid.

"I'm not sure exactly what I would do, Mom, but I would try to protect her. Yell, throw rocks, run at the animal if nothing else works, who knows?"

"Oh God," mom said. "You probably would, given how you threw yourself at that dog when you were a small child. I'm lucky I didn't die of heart failure on the spot. I thought you'd be a little wiser now that you're an adult, and with a wild animal, no less."

When I was seven years old, the large boxer from across the street attacked our tiny Chihuahua, Randy. He had our little dog pinned against the neighbors' house. I threw open the screen door, ran at full speed, and hurled my body into the boxer while my mother screamed helplessly after me to stop. I so surprised the boxer that when he regained his balance, he simply walked away with a bewildered look and went home. Randy was fine—just a bit shaken. Not smart, I agree, but my instinct was to protect Randy.

A few moments later, I hear an interchange between my mom and dad that makes me grateful for how well Tom and I *do* communicate.

Perhaps our human relationships are inevitably conflicted. As such, there is a great potential to grow from them. But that growth can be difficult and painful. The beauty of Maggie, and perhaps all well-adjusted dogs, is that love with them is *not* conflicted. Their love is pure and innocent no matter what our flaws. Her unrelenting love and acceptance of me is the fountain that rejuvenates me and gives me the strength to try again in my human relationships. It leads me back to forgive and love myself. From there, it expresses outward. I often wonder if animals, like children, are life's gift to us to rekindle our own link with purity and innocence.

"Ah, if only humans were more like dogs; what a wonderful world this would be," says Tom's dad when he sweetly pets Maggie's head.

The individual patterns that create conflict between Tom and me are hard to shift entirely. We are committed, however, to understand each other's viewpoint once we calm down. That's where we find understanding, even if we don't have agreement.

After one such disharmonious interaction, Tom finds me in our bedroom hugging Maggie. He holds his hands out to me and enfolds me in his arms. "You two are so bonded that I feel like the third wheel sometimes. Maggie is *your* dog much more than she is *our* dog."

It's true. Yet I think it's bigger than simply Maggie and I spending more time together. There is a depth and connection we share that feels larger than both of us. Perhaps like the bond between a mother and her child. When I stumble to and from the bathroom during the night, half asleep, her tail thumps wildly as I walk by. It feels as though Maggie has always been a part of me and that she *always will be*. In this strange way, I think I take her and the ever-present consistency of her love for granted.

Maggie gives herself into life with abandon. She isn't concerned about protecting herself from pain and disappointment. She keeps not an ounce of her love in check. Her authenticity serves as my reminder that we are all unique with our own divine spark. Being my genuine self as fully as possible and bringing that spark out like Maggie does seems to be a large part of what life is about—since there's only one of each of us. I begin to wonder if our animals mirror for us the qualities and lessons we need to learn.

The winter brings shocking news to our family. Tom Jr. and Scott's mother, Sharon, dies unexpectedly in her sleep. She was only forty-four years old. The immediate cause was a potassium deficiency that she learned about the day before when she collapsed from extreme weakness at work. Her doctor tried to keep her hospitalized until her levels returned to normal. She refused. Even though the doctor explained the danger to her heart, she left the hospital against medical advice and spent the night at her boyfriend's house. He awakened to her dead beside him the next morning. The secondary cause of death was liver disease due to her alcoholism. What a blow to Tom's sons.

Even though the boys, particularly Tom Jr., have a lot of anger toward their mother, this loss is very traumatic for them. The day after Sharon's funeral, Tom and I long to experience the consolation and beauty only nature can offer. We walk with Maggie in stunned silence along the Sanitas Valley trail. It's cloaked in fresh snow. The hills and trees glisten in the sunlight. Maggie rolls in the snow—which energizes her even more than water—and kicks her feet in the air. She provides such a lovely contrast to sorrow as we try to come to grips with such a preventable death. Maggie leaps up and catches the snowballs tossed her way, zooms back and forth in front of us, then up and down the trail. She tucks her hind-end under her and scrambles across the snow. I call it her tail-tuck-and-run. Thank heaven for the joy of a dog. Her celebration of snow during this somber time is a gift.

Although Tom Jr. had a few major bumps in the road dealing with his anger and drinking prior to his mom's untimely death, seeing "cirrhosis of the liver" listed on his mother's death certificate is his turning point. Drinking becomes a non-issue from this point forward, other than a couple of beers at a baseball game or occasionally with his friends. He graduates with a business degree and sets his sights on how to live a positive, fulfilling life.

Scott goes the other direction. The high school friends he drank with outgrow it. They move on into jobs they like and develop relationships. Some of them tell Scott point-blank that he is going to follow in his mother's footsteps if he doesn't change. Scott ignores them. His car insurance remains prohibitive, so he gives up driving rather than drinking since the threat of jail frightens him. Thank God for the innocents on the road. There is no talking to Scott. He denies and blames. Nothing is ever his fault. Of course *he* doesn't have a problem.

"Just like Sharon," Tom says. Although it breaks his heart, he feels more and more helpless and out of control as to how to help Scott, as is true of so many family members of alcoholics. Both of us are learning to let go of trying to change Scott, especially Tom as he struggles to come to terms with Scott's choices and find his own peace of mind.

I observed Tom be sort of a tough guy with his sons during their late-adolescent wrestling matches. Yet he's a man with so much love to give—a real tender-hearted person. So it warms me to watch Maggie coax Tom's softness out in his treatment of her. On most nights, she follows him downstairs to hang out with him while he does his yoga stretches and grabs some time to himself.

Often, I hear him singing to her, "Oh Magster-Wagster, oh Magster-Wagster, prettiest girl in town, prettiest girl in town ..."

Even with the ever-present wound of knowing we can't impact a loved one in pain, our life goes on. There's so much life to live: fourteeners to climb, hikes to discover, travels that call to us, family and friends to share life with—and in the winter, movies to be seen. Oh yes, we *love* movies. If I had it all to do again, I think I'd love to be involved in the creative process of making movies.

When Tom and I return from a Friday-night movie, Maggie thunders downstairs to greet us with unbridled enthusiasm at the garage door. We can hear her feet tap dancing as we place the key in the door. We enter. Back and forth she runs in the family room, pants with excitement, and naturally engages in my favorite—her tail-tuck-and-run. Then she turns in frivolous circles with a wild gleam in her eyes. Cinnamon is right on her haunches but stays out of the way while Maggie performs her happy dance.

"She is just so alive," I remark. Tom stands and smiles at

me.

"What?" I ask, knowing his smile is saying more.

"Like someone else I know," he winks at me. We saunter up the stairs.

"You think so, huh?"

"Absolutely! That's what attracted me to you, you know. Well, after those hazel eyes, your thick, brown, wavy hair, and your tight little body. Your physical beauty wouldn't have been enough to hold me, though. It was your *zest* for life that drew me," Tom reveals.

"Really? I don't think I ever knew that part," I tell him.

"You loved *doing* things, especially outdoors. You windsurfed, hiked, biked, and skied. You liked to camp, travel, and dance—and still do. You enjoyed people and laughed a lot. You and Maggie are so much alike!"

I consider this as we crawl into bed. I love the comparison. But am I still this alive? It seems I let life bog me down a bit. Especially since I went back to get my master's degree. I'm more serious. Do I laugh less? Have a little less fun?

Our lovemaking has a peculiar facet to it with Maggie around. With pleasurable sounds emanating from our bed, I open my eyes to find myself staring directly into Maggie's smiling, inquiring eyes. Seconds later, Tom is rudely nudged by a cold nose from behind. Her tail wags her entire body. Is Maggie really concerned about the sounds, or does she simply feel the energy of love and want to be close to it?

Maggie seems to sense the importance of her job, that of bringing joy and laughter to us. *Her* aliveness serves as our constant reminder to lighten up and stay in touch with our own. Yet I have been getting bogged down, missing her reminders at times.

She is so interwoven into the fabric of our lives that it's easy to take for granted that she will always be there. I can't begin to imagine life without her greeting.

Chapter Seven
Life Is a Big Buffet

I graduate from my master's program in 1996. But my studying doesn't end. Now, practicing as a family nurse practitioner, I diagnose and treat patients in a family practice clinic. I feel my school program didn't adequately prepare me for the magnitude of knowledge I need to practice. So I continue to immerse myself in study to broaden my knowledge in the health care field. I definitely overwork my left brain with the steady diet of intellectualism I feed it. With the ever-changing field of medicine, I'm not sure I see an end to studying.

Once again, I don't fit comfortably in the role. Yet other nurse practitioners and doctors don't appear to struggle with it as I do. Why? I don't like to hurry with my patients. I want to listen fully to their health concerns to get the whole picture in order to diagnose and treat them appropriately. But managed health care is aimed toward seeing large numbers of patients and getting them out as quickly as possible. I am not good at being quick in my health-care delivery. Am I just too much of a perfectionist, expecting too much of myself? Perhaps so, but certain aspects of the health care system are just plain disturbing. For example, new drugs are continually released by pharmaceutical companies and approved by the FDA as safe. Some of these are drugs I prescribe. I'm disturbed when some are later taken off the market because of their detrimental effects.

Between work and my ongoing continuing education, I am

constantly busy. I neglect my intuition and creativity (my right brain), with the exception of my dream work. I have been seeing a Jungian therapist, who guides me in deciphering the unconscious messages offered through my dream symbolism. I barely find time even for this, but it feels vital to my soul that I continue. Maggie comes with me and lays at my feet during our sessions, front paws crossed in her usual fashion. It seems she will always lie at my side, a part of everything.

Our holiday celebrations and family gatherings are fuller for us with Maggie present. In June 1997, Tom Jr. marries Fabiola, a lovely young woman from Mexico who he's been with for the past couple of years. We hold their wedding and reception at our home. The caterer sets up the food buffet in front of the house, along with tables and chairs under tents. After dinner, people scatter and circulate onto the back deck and into the house. I'm busy being the hostess. Maggie runs through the crowd and visits everyone, and suddenly Tom notices she's gone. He searches for her and finds her at the long buffet table. She is standing on her hind legs with her large paws on the table. Miss Magster-Wagster is working her way down the line of food from left to right. With no one there to stop her, she hit the jackpot. Then Tom shows up. Maggie turns and looks at him with her "oh-oh" expression. Food is smeared all over her mouth. Tom can't stop laughing as he is relaying this to me.

The caterers bag all the trash before they leave. We place the plastic bags at the end of our driveway. During the night, raccoons tear into the trash bags. Tom lets Maggie outside the next morning to do her business. She doesn't return to the door, which is not at all like her. Tom looks for her but doesn't have to go far. He finds her at the end of the driveway—going for seconds—with her head in the middle of a big trash bag.

"Maggie!" She jerks her head up in surprise at his stern voice and looks at Tom. Her entire face is white from the sour cream treasure she just unburied. Busted again. Tom calls me to see. Even though we know we're probably in for a night of dog diarrhea, all we can do is laugh. These are the unpredictable moments with her that stand out, that put their own stamp on our history together and tighten the bond among the three of us.

About the only events Maggie isn't part of are when Tom and I leave the country on vacation or go on our summer mountain trip to Lake City. She and Cinnamon stay home with a house sitter. I spend so much time with Maggie that I am like a parent needing a break from a child. As Maggie's primary caregiver, I want this time to be free of responsibility and to just spend it with Tom. I need a vacation from the daily tasks and routine. That is about to change.

Chapter Eight
Our Bubble Bursts

*T*om, Maggie and I are driving to a local craft fair. It's fall. I look in the rearview mirror and catch Maggie watching me intently from the backseat the way she does. What is she thinking as she stares at me? Her eyes reflect a wisdom and awareness that seems so un-doglike. I reach back and place my hand on her paws. She bathes it thoroughly with warm kisses.

We come across a woman at the fair who carves and paints wooden animals. A smiling dog with angel wings catches my eye. I stop dead in my tracks when I read the inscription, "What pure joy she was." *Was.* Shivers travel up my spine. I know the day will come when I will have to buy that piece. I can't bear the thought.

"I love your art. It's so unique. You have obviously lost a dog you dearly loved."

"It was my dog's death that inspired this work," she replies.

I look at Maggie. She is doing her little pounce off the ground with her front legs, trying to get the woman to notice her. I swallow hard. Will that happen for me, too, that Maggie's passing will somehow inspire my passion and creativity? I can't go there.

"You can be that special black Labrador retriever who lives until you're twenty years old, Mags," I tell her again that night before my shower when she comes up from the family room. She parks against the bathtub. I squat next to her before I step in the shower and stroke her head. Our eyes meet and hold. It's rare for a dog to hold such extended eye contact. I lose myself in her depth, and it startles me to experience such a powerful spiritual connection with a dog. I am deeply moved by the intensity of love pouring forth from her eyes to mine and back again. In magical moments such as these, the windows to our souls meet. I often ponder, "Who *are* you in there?"

As I bustle through the house and yard with daily chores, my little princess is at my side. She plops down. Her eyes drink in my every move and await my next one. My mom calls her my "constant companion."

In early December, Maggie rolls ritualistically on her back in our bedroom and invites her daily belly rub. That's when I notice it—the small, raised bump on her left chest. I think it's a cyst, and I'm not too concerned. I wait until after Christmas to make an appointment with Pet Care 24 Clinic to have it checked. Dr. Gordon, Maggie's vet, isn't there. This clinic pulled Shanna through her crisis when we thought we were going to lose her—I trust them.

I haven't met Dr. Lincoln before. She aspirates the lesion with a needle to observe the cells under a microscope. I'm not at all prepared when she returns to the exam room and announces her findings.

"It's a mast cell tumor, a type of cancer. Some are slow growing, but some are very aggressive and spread rapidly to other organs." Maggie is only eight years old. This can't be!

"You caught it early, so it's less likely to have spread to other body organs yet," she goes on. "But we need to schedule her for surgery tomorrow. We'll send the tissue to cytology to determine what grade the tumor is. Grade-one cancers have the best prognosis with less chance of metastasis (spread to other parts of the body). Grade-two and-three tumors are more aggressive."

Cancer? Surgery *tomorrow?* I'm in shock. Her urgency and decisiveness are sobering. But her emphatic direction leaves me in no doubt about our course of action. I schedule her surgery for tomorrow with Dr. Gordon. My drive home to deliver this unexpected blow to Tom is a blur. I am thankful it is one of the two days a week he works at home. He is as dazed and shaken as I am.

At 7:00 AM, we sulk into the exam room. Maggie bursts through the doorway and wags her tail with her usual grand entrance.

"What adventure awaits me here?" her curious expression asks. The world is her oyster, even at the vet's office. After all, there are people and dogs to greet and treats to be had. We meet briefly with Dr. Gordon and are thankful for her warm, cheerful confidence.

"I will have to make a wide, deep incision to be sure we get clean margins," Dr. Gordon explains, meaning the entire tumor has to be removed with no cells left behind for new growth to seed from. "The incisions from mast cell tumors have a tendency to come apart because of the histamine this type of tumor releases. So I want her to be a couch potato when she goes home. No activity."

How are we going to keep Maggie *quiet?*

I swallow hard. She will be in pain. The possibility that she might have cancer elsewhere in her body is more than I can bear. We have to live with that unknown now.

I wrap my arms around my black beauty queen. "Don't forget our twenty-year plan, baby love." My hope for a long life together is crumbling.

"Maggie has only been in a kennel once in her life, when she had her teeth cleaned," I tell Dr. Gordon. "She went nuts. Please don't put her in a kennel before or after surgery, Dr. Gordon. Promise me." I am so frightened to leave her alone in someone else's hands to undergo surgery and anesthesia.

"No problem. We'll tie her outside of the kennel with a blanket on the floor to recover her, and a vet technician will be in the room at all times," Dr. Gordon assures me. "I'll give you an update if you want to call at 11:00 AM. You can pick her up at 7:00 PM tonight."

A twelve-hour wait. This is difficult for me. When our human loved ones have surgery, we stay at the hospital and wait. The doctor comes and talks to us as soon as surgery is over. We get to be with them in the recovery room. Offer support. Follow them to their room. Receive assurance by seeing that they are okay. Get updates from their nurse. I so want to stay with Maggie and support her. But the way that veterinary clinics are set up, that's not feasible without being in the way of the staff.

I can't be with her, but I do trust she'll get the best care. The diagnostic tests and treatment for animals in our country in a good vet clinic are on a par with human health care, limited only by our bank accounts and our pets' inability to tell us their symptoms.

Tom leaves the clinic for work. Walking out without Maggie leaves me empty. I am thankful for my good friend, Anne. She knows the depth of my bond with Maggie and how upset I am. She meets me at the clinic.

"Where do you want to hike, Dawnie?" she asks with affection.

"I don't care, Anne," I say. Hiking is therapeutic for me. It helps me get my mind off my fears. I'm still reeling from the cancer diagnosis. I pray Maggie will make it through surgery, that it is a grade-one tumor, and that we found it early enough.

"How about the Sanitas Valley Trail?" suggests Anne.

How appropriate. As we walk, I envision Maggie's inviting expression as she approaches people. The way her tail wags in a circle. The goofy way she tucks her behind and runs, especially in snow.

The day drags. Will 7:00 PM ever arrive? I can't wait to see her. Hug her. Comfort her. Feel her warm tongue on my face. And bring her home. When we finally walk into the back room where Maggie lays on a blanket, we're in for another shock. I expect to see the Maggie I know, but with less energy. She was spayed as a pup and bounced back after surgery as though nothing happened. Now she is in a stupor, barely able to stand. I didn't realize she would still be so drugged. The Fentanyl patch on her right side to ease her pain is partly the culprit. She gives a brief tail thump. Other than that, she shows minimal interest in us. Her face is blank. Maggie just simply isn't "home."

On the ride home, Maggie's entire countenance droops. Her head hangs low, and she drools. The Maggie spirit we know is not present. At home, she sleeps, oblivious to her surroundings. Seeing her so unlike herself unnerves us. My stomach is in knots. Tom and I go to bed very disturbed. I finally fall into a restless sleep with Maggie settled at the foot of our bed.

At 3:00 AM, I awaken to a cold, wet nose nuzzling my face. My eyes meet Maggie's twinkling in the moonlight. My baby girl is returning! She never awakened me at night before. Although not fully herself yet, I sense she awakened me to let me know, "Mom, I'm here. I'm okay. Don't worry anymore!" I am relieved and fall into a peaceful slumber.

But the next several days reveal that my angel is far from out of the woods. Her movements are stiff and effortful. Her hips lag when she rises. The surgery was so much more of an insult than we expected, both to her body and her mood. Although Maggie remains sweet and receptive to our attention, she's withdrawn, pulled into herself for the first time in her life. My thinking that she would bounce back like she did after her spay was so wrong. Her recovery is slow and painful.

Ten days pass. Maggie and I go in for her follow-up visit with Dr. Gordon. Thankfully, it was a grade-one tumor. Dr. Gordon warns me that mast cell tumors often return. "One dog had twelve recurrences and twelve surgeries in two years."

Twelve? The thought of Maggie enduring even *one* more surgery like this terrifies me. I'm determined this will not be her fate.

Chapter Nine
What's Really Best for
Our Pets?

With our world rocked, I begin exploring new directions. I am on a mission to find some answers and make necessary changes. In the holistic pet care section of the Boulder Bookstore, I immerse myself in reading about animal health problems, the roots of their causes, and alternative practices through the eyes of holistically oriented veterinary healers. I hope to discover possible causes of Maggie's mast cell cancer and what we might do to prevent a recurrence.

Cancer is becoming more common in dogs, I learn. Animals that lived to age fifteen or sixteen in the 1960s now die at seven or eight.[1] Arthritis and hip dysplasia are becoming rampant.[2] Maggie was diagnosed with arthritis in her elbow joint at age seven.

Why are these degenerative diseases on the rise in our canines? I discover some eye-opening facts about diet.

We have the difficult realization that we didn't provide Maggie with the healthiest diet during these eight years. We were taught, as most of us were, that dog food was nutritionally balanced, and table food was not good for animals. We fed her a popular brand, recommended by most veterinarians. I learn it contains chemical preservatives, and much of its protein comes from grain rather than meat sources. Had I known that the amount of nutrition education veterinary schools provide is even less than what doctors receive in medical school, I would have explored a better diet for Maggie much sooner. Most veterinarians are taught that dog food is the best diet for our canine best friends. The dog food industry representatives educate veterinarians about their foods in much the same way that pharmaceutical representatives educate physicians, physician assistants, and nurse practitioners about new drugs. How many drugs are recalled after causing significant human damage and even death? Unfortunately, well-meaning health care professionals and veterinarians who we trust are at the effect of the profit motivated pharmaceutical and pet food industries. How are we, the consumers, to know what to believe?

Diet and nutrition is linked to human cancers and numerous other ailments. Why would animals be any different? What I discover about the dog food industry and its practices is nothing short of appalling.

I read that many pet foods contain inadequate quantities and qualities of proteins, fats, vitamins, and minerals. Most labels only list the amount of *crude* protein. Many consumers don't realize that the digestion and absorption is very different for different proteins. Many manufacturers use inexpensive sources such as poultry feathers, fecal waste, and horse and cattle hair that provide pets with significantly less *usable* protein. Vitamins, minerals, and amino acids added to pet food are often destroyed by heat processing and during shelf storage.[3]

Another shock was learning that the pet food industry is built on remnants rejected by the human food industry. This can mean slaughterhouse wastes such as spoiled meats and even tissues riddled with cancer. These discards also include moldy grains and rancid fats.[4] As if this isn't bad enough, many pet foods contain "fillers, heavy-metal contaminants, sugar, pesticides, herbicides, drug residues, artificial colors, flavors, and preservatives."[5] Vitamins and enzymes are essential to detoxify and eliminate toxins and pollutants such as these. Yet it's these same contaminants that deplete the body of those very vitamins and enzymes.[6] As of this writing, we are in the midst of an unprecedented major pet food recall due to tainted wheat gluten and rice protein with the toxin melamine.

I research further into problems associated with just one of the above discards—moldy grains. I learn they can produce mycotoxins, the poisonous residues of mold deterioration. These are very potent compounds that cause a variety of human and animal health problems at very low dosages. Aflatoxin, one of several mycotoxins, is a potent carcinogen and immunosuppressant. It was found to be responsible for the mysterious deaths of one hundred thousand turkeys in England; this is when mycotoxin poisoning was first discovered. Other animal and human effects of aflatoxin include intestinal hemorrhage, liver degeneration, and cancer acceleration. Grains often affected include corn, peanuts, wheat, and rice,[7] all of which are used in various dog foods.

Pet food manufacturers in most states are *allowed* to use dead or diseased animal tissues. P. F. McGargle, DVM and federal meat inspector, concluded that the slaughterhouse wastes in pet food increases the chances of animal cancer and other degenerative diseases.[8]

Dr. Pitcairn believes the chemical additives in pet food also play a major part in the decline in pet health that he has seen since he began practicing in 1965.[9]

I investigate two of the chemical additives in Maggie's dry dog food. The first, butylated hydroxyanisole (BHA), was shown to be carcinogenic in experimental rats, Syrian Golden hamsters, and mice when administered in the diet, according to the Report on Carcinogens, Eleventh Edition.[10] The second, ethoxyquin, is often used to stabilize fats in dog food—it's also a pesticide—and is suspected of being a cancer-causing agent. After a scientific review of a study from the Monsanto

Company, the Food and Drug Administration's (FDA) Center for Veterinary Medicine (CVM) believes the 150 parts per million (ppm) that regulations allow may not be safe for lactating dogs and puppies. The CVM requested the allowable level be lowered to 75 ppm.[11]

Dr. Gordon's words from our follow-up visit still ring in my ears and are incredulous to me. "Why are you going to change her diet? She's done so well on it all these years."

How can she overlook a possible link between Maggie's cancer and her nutrition? Even human Western medicine is relating diet to cancer and other diseases.

There is no question that we are going to change Maggie's diet. Dr. Pitcairn's book has several recipes in it, but I want direct guidance by someone local regarding what food and supplements to give Maggie and in what proportions.

I also plan to take Maggie for acupuncture to help her recover from the insult of such an intense surgery. Acupuncture is a 3,500-year-old Chinese practice of inserting small needles into specific points along the body's meridians, the channels through which energy flows in the body, to stimulate healing. Acupuncture can correct excesses or deficiencies of energy by manipulating these points. According to Chinese medicine, energy imbalances cause illnesses, and correcting those imbalances can cure them.[12] I hope to help heal whatever imbalances Maggie's body might have that allowed cancer in the first place. In my practice as a nurse practitioner, I try to integrate the best of Western medicine with alternative therapies with my patients. I refer them for acupuncture if I think it might help them with chronic ailments. I had acupuncture myself on more than one occasion and found it beneficial. I also believe in an integrated approach for my animals. At the time I learned that Maggie had arthritis, I was informed that the drug used to treat it in dogs, Rimadyl, has an adverse effect on the liver of black Labradors, often resulting in death. Rimadyl is not an option for Maggie. The only other option at the time was aspirin (ibuprofen is toxic to dogs). I planned to take her for acupuncture for her arthritis when it became necessary.

During the first week after surgery, I take Maggie to the Brewing Market for mental stimulation and diversion since she can't exercise. She lays next to my chair and waves her tail but is less enthusiastic than usual. Her eyes catch the passersby. People naturally stop to visit her. Many who know her and other dog lovers ask, "Why does she have a T-shirt on?"

"We have to protect her incision," I explain. The news of her mast cell cancer saddens those who know her.

This leads to interactions with several people who speak of having their own dogs on a raw food diet at the recommendation of Dr. Rupp, a well-known holistic vet in Boulder. He also does acupuncture. Bingo. I found my local holistic vet. It takes a few weeks to get an appointment with him.

I look up to observe a tall blond man walk in the exam room. Handsome and with a nice build, he has a very slight accent—Austrian roots, I learn. I wonder how Maggie will respond to the needles. She doesn't take kindly to the automatic table that elevates from the floor to Dr. Rupp's level. Her eyes search the floor and between Dr. Rupp and me for her escape. A few points must be sensitive, since Maggie jerks as the needles go in. For most of the needle insertions, however, she doesn't flinch. But she takes us both by surprise when she suddenly leaps off the table toward a squirrel outside the exam room window. Luckily, Dr. Rupp reacts instantly and catches her in mid-air! I doubt that his back appreciates this move. Once he has needles placed at various points around her body, he lowers the table and leaves us alone for thirty minutes to let the needles do their work while he goes to see another patient. Maggie paces around the small room for a brief time. I'm amazed at how well the needles stay in. After just a few minutes, she relaxes. She lies down, and a peaceful calm settles over her. She even sleeps. This relaxation stays with her the remainder of the day.

Maggie's level of energy the day after her treatment is another story. Her step has a bounce. Her expression is brighter and happier. With more pep, she is ready to play again. I take Maggie to Dr. Rupp for weekly acupuncture for two months, at which time he feels it is fine to decrease it to once a month. Even the slight limp she developed in her left front leg disappears for several weeks after treatment. It only begins to creep back in just days before her next acupuncture appointment. When we add daily glucosamine sulfate to her regimen, the limp completely disappears.

I continue my quest for causes. What I learn about breeding practices and vaccinations startles me.

Breeding practices have affected the gene pool, resulting in health problems. Selective breeding over thousands of generations created new lines of dogs of every size and purpose. This selective breeding has led to unique behaviors and appearances. It's also led to increased congenital defects and malfunctions. Breeding for desired traits such as floppy ears may be a trade-off for future compromised health, such as chronic ear infections.

To assure that a cute or unique characteristic, such as short legs, appears consistently, inbreeding must occur. Such inbreeding between siblings or parents and offspring might perpetuate inherited diseases and other weaknesses, such as low stamina and poor resistance to disease. The bottom line is that dogs are not bred for their health and comfort. Many of them suffer as a consequence. Statistics predict that 10 to 25 percent of each litter may be born defective. Most breeders just accept this fact.[13]

Animal vaccinations are the next belief system I raise the

curtain on. We were overvaccinating our pets, a problem many veterinarians now recognize. The yearly booster shots recommended by most vets have little justification. Journals report diseases that follow routine vaccinations.[14] These include "bleeding disorders, bone and joint inflammation, even tumors and cancers."[15] Vaccinations may cause acute diseases or chronic health problems such as skin allergies, hyperthyroidism, lupus, and inflammatory bowel problems. These immune system disorders may result more from *combination* vaccines that overwhelm and confuse the immune system. Dr. Pitcairn recommends *single* vaccines instead of delivering several at once. He also advises a reduced vaccination schedule for young animals. He believes that immunizing puppies (and kittens) protects them for several years and possibly for a lifetime. Waiting until sixteen weeks of age may do less harm to its immune system.[16]

I vaccinated Maggie yearly all of her life, thinking it contributed to her health. I feel weak when I read that "giving a vaccine to an animal with cancer is like pouring gasoline on a fire."[17] She had received her *last* vaccination, with the exception of the rabies vaccine, which is required by law every three years.

So how did veterinarians come to believe that combined vaccinations *every* year were necessary? Was their education too one-sided? Too influenced by representatives of the vaccine manufacturers? Perhaps vets saw one too many cases of parvo virus that a vaccine might have prevented. Because of the infectious diseases vaccines are designed to prevent, the decision to further vaccinate or not after puppy immunizations is not straightforward. It's something I'm still unclear about and will continue to research.

Dr. Rupp spends a good hour with me during that first visit discussing the ingredients and proper proportions of a raw food diet. He gives me a handout to refer to. We begin cooking for Maggie. Her new diet consists of raw ground turkey, vegetables, grains, and beans. We add vitamin supplements and a nutritional powder of kelp, nutritional yeast, bone meal, and lecithin. What a project!

Dr. Rupp also diagnoses Maggie with hypothyroidism and places her on thyroid-replacement medication. He will test her blood levels of thyroid hormone every few months to be sure she gets the proper amount and adjust her dosage accordingly.

The diet change is worth the trouble. It adds energy and exuberance to Maggie's already abundant supply. Her coat develops a shine and luster that becomes the topic of many conversations with people she stops in their tracks. After eight years of constant shedding, it just suddenly stops—a result of her new diet I didn't expect but am very pleased with. I learn that the condition of a dog's coat tells much about their state of health. I'm sad to admit that during her eight years of eating a well-known and highly recommended brand of dog food, Maggie's coat was dull and she shed continually.

There are now several brands of high-quality pet foods made with *human-grade* protein as the first ingredient and without by-products or chemical preservatives. These can be found at smaller holistic pet food stores and include brands such as Canidae, Innova, Natural Balance, and Chicken Soup for the Dog Lovers Soul, among others. Flint River Ranch products can be ordered online.

Recover Maggie does. Her quality of life surpasses her presurgery level. She maintains her new energy level. We are all about to enter the best times of our lives together. Oh, and Maggie never has a mast cell tumor recurrence.

Chapter Ten
You Light Up My Life

I wake up with that feeling again. It's new in the last few weeks. I was never sad about not having children before, but I am now. It's a sense of loss. I am acutely aware that my biological window for having children is closing. It had always been *my* choice before. Now my body is the ultimate decision maker. I'll never have a child of my own—never be a mother. A major experience I missed as a woman. I can almost feel the daughter I didn't have. I sense the nurturing, loving relationship that could have been. *Never* is such a sobering word.

Maybe my view of having children versus life outside the home was too narrow. A lot of moms balance working outside the home with raising children. Or maybe I simply don't like that life and age are removing the choice that was mine until now. I've always been one who needs to leave my options open, so I don't feel trapped. Limiting, I know. As a nurse, I often worked per diem, giving up benefits so *when* I worked was in my control. As a nurse practitioner, I worked on contract or like now, I have my own practice. I did the same as a psychotherapist. Did my strong need to hang on to control come from feeling overly controlled and with little choice as a child?

I ponder the many life experiences I readily chose that may not have been as easy to do as a mother: volunteering with an optometry group to fit hundreds of the poor and underserved in Durango, Mexico, with donated eyeglasses; driving two days to volunteer in an animal shelter during a hurricane-relief effort; windsurfing with Tom numerous times in South Padre Island and the Columbia River Gorge; exploring Costa Rica, New Zealand, Tahiti, Hawaii, Mexico, Vancouver Island, and the Washington/Oregon coast together; traveling with friends to Peru, Ecuador, and the Galapagos Islands; experiencing both the beauty and the deprivation of Third World culture in Guatemala and sharing the trip with Heather; coming face to face with the incredible gray whales in Baja's San Ignacio Lagoon in Mexico when they swam under and up to our boat. It was a connection with another being so powerful and extraordinary that it expanded my ties with life in a new way. These experiences enriched me and helped mold the clay that created the sculpture of who I am today.

I'm jolted out of my thoughts by a cold, wet nose poking my hand, as though to remind me of her place in my life. I smile at her. Maggie is like my child, and she, too, is enriching and molding who I am becoming. With the depth of love I have for her, could I have loved a child more? I know the answer is yes. Yet my focus turns to Maggie now more than ever. My sadness about the finality of not having children seems to be more about feelings I need to come to grips with and let go of.

Maggie's mast cell tumor is a wakeup call for Tom and me. She won't always be here. We no longer take our girl for granted. We are viewing her through a different lens. Her mortality becomes a reality to us that we never entertained before. We take more pictures of her. We treat each day as though it's her last—a lesson I can take into all of my relationships. Even the daily routine with her holds new meaning. We make fun out of small events.

For example, neither Tom nor I are big TV watchers, but we pick one program to watch together on Thursday nights. We make it an event. Popcorn is a must. Maggie has no complaints about that. The moment she hears the popcorn dropping into the popper, she flies into the kitchen and stares at it until it finishes popping. Tom and I sit on the couch with the popcorn bowl. Maggie sits several feet away, watching and waiting. For the next hour, we toss one piece at a time into the air for her to catch. Magster loves the game as much as the popcorn. We treasure these moments as Maggie slips—almost unnoticed by us—from the prime of her life into her early golden years.

We begin taking her on most errands into town. When we go to the health club, Home Depot, Costco, or out to eat, Maggie waits for us in the car. Our relationship with her blossoms even more beautifully. Life was certainly *simpler* before we started taking Maggie everywhere with us, especially since we live several miles out of town. Prior to taking her, we didn't have to worry about leaving her in a hot car or making an extra trip to take her home because it was too hot. But life is certainly *richer* having her with us more.

Yet we do tire of the homemade dog food project. It seems overwhelming at times. But we continue because it seems the best nutrition for her. But there must be an easier way....

Maggie accompanies me to appointments in dog-friendly places, which there are plenty of in Boulder. After she greets my chiropractor or massage therapist with a big wiggle and a wag, Maggie curls up under the massage table and quietly waits for me. She occasionally sticks her cold, wet nose up through the face cradle or up against my ear just to check in and give me a lick.

She is a hit with all the stylists at Zumo's, where I have my hair cut. She roams through the beauty shop and visits the other stylists and their clients. She usually ends up in the kitchen, where the stylists keep their dog treats. Finally, she parks next to my chair and waits for me. When I see my Jungian therapist each month for dream interpretation, Maggie is privy to my inner world.

One day, Maggie and I stop by Glenda's optometry office to donate eyeglasses for her yearly trip to Mexico. Her dog, Axie, often spends her day in the tiny yard outside of the office. Maggie adores Axie and revs up into play mode the moment she sees her. Maggie runs back-and-forth in her legendary butt tuck. On one of her passes, Maggie unexpectedly explodes, wide-eyed, through the open office door. She ignores my command to come—probably her worst trait, and my biggest training error. I follow on her heels in my futile attempt to stop her. The faces of the patients and office staff register disbelief and confusion at Maggie's sudden jubilant entrance; then smiles creep in and replace their surprise. Maggie is on a mission. To my dismay, she bursts through Glenda's exam room door while she is examining a patient. Glenda loves Maggie, but my friend is none too pleased with this little outburst in her professional setting. I apologize profusely, extremely embarrassed. Once Glenda's patient leaves, however, even she is chuckling.

I often see people in town who know Maggie but don't know my name. On the trail, Maggie entices approaching hikers. She wags her tail in circles and her eyes speak to them. "Hi! It's me. I'm happy to see you! You want to hang out with me a bit, right? We'll both be happier if we do. Aren't you loving being out here?"

"What a beautiful dog!" They greet her in return. "You can just tell by looking at her that she's so sweet!"

She nuzzles her moist nose into the faces of small children when they cross her path. With the gentle look of a loving mother, her pink tongue covers their faces like a washrag as the children giggle with glee.

When we travel by car now, Maggie goes with us. From long weekend winter excursions to extended summer mountain trips, Maggie embarks on the adventure, too. No more leaving her home with the house sitter. Our favorite trip with her is to the beautiful Colorado mountain town of Crested Butte, appropriately nicknamed the "wildflower capital of the world." Surrounded by the Maroon Bells-Snowmass and Raggeds Wilderness, this paradise holds us in its arms during the month of July, when the wildflowers peak and snowmelt feeds abundant streams.

Maggie's shiny black beauty provides lovely contrast among the medley of colors exploding in "God's Garden." The term *Hiking in Heaven*—a popular hiking book here—aptly describes our favorite trails in Rustler's Gulch and West Maroon Pass. The waist-high, lavender columbine, rosy paintbrush, and velvet purple monkshood intoxicate us, as do so many other vibrant flower varieties and colors. Maggie thrives in this land of cooler temperatures and running streams, where she cools her sun-soaked coat with delight.

Luckily, hotels are becoming pet-friendly. When we are

unable to rent a condominium in Crested Butte, we stay in the pet wing at the Sheraton Hotel. It's comical to watch Maggie plaster her nose under every door crack as each room erupts in a chorus of barking. She loves trotting past the front desk and visiting people in the hotel lobby.

Once we return home, however, Maggie and I hike and walk less together. It is hard to leave Maggie watching in her uncomprehending way at the front door as I walk away without her. Upon my return, she is still there, waiting. Her tail bangs the floor as I come into view. When I start up the steps toward the front door, she begins prancing, lifting her legs alternately like a filly doing dressage.

Tom and I take her swimming more often now to avoid impact on her joints. It also keeps her cooler in the summer since her black coat, which is developing a red sheen, seems to sizzle in the heat of the sun. Besides, water is her love.

Maggie is definitely maturing. The top of her head is losing its smooth appearance, and her face is dropping ever so slightly. But so is mine. She finally has a few gray hairs under her chin, but they are barely visible. Is this reddening of her coat due to the sun? Why hasn't it happened before? Perhaps it's related to her diet change. I hope she isn't getting too much or too little of an essential nutrient.

Her face still maintains a youthful appearance. When people stop to pet her and ask her age, they are surprised when we tell them she's nearly nine years old. Retrieving balls from the lake is now a love rather than a crazed obsession. Thank God. She moves just a little slower. Although Maggie maintains her enthusiasm and playfulness with people and activity, calm is her new baseline. It just sort of sneaked in the back door.

"An older dog is like a fine wine," a woman at the Brewing Market comments. "They just get better with age."

Oh, that they do, my friend, that they do.

Chapter Eleven
Warnings from the Soul

*I*n April 2000, Tom, Maggie and I make the lengthy drive to South Padre Island once again at the end of tax season to windsurf. Maggie hasn't been there with us for nearly nine years. I can't wait to see her excitement at being in the ocean again.

We need the fun and relaxation this trip always gives us. Tom is exhausted after the stress of yet another intense tax season. I've been working as a nurse practitioner for four years now. It *still* doesn't quite fit me. I'm becoming aware that I'm working more under a persona that allows me to function in our health care system. I am feeling like a fish out of water, but I'm not yet ready to admit to myself that perhaps this line of work is not my soul's calling. I left the family practice clinic six months ago after three-and-a-half years. Now I have my own practice in a women's clinic that integrates alternative therapies into our practices. Not only do I continue spending much of my free time staying current on the swiftly changing medical field; I am also staying current on nutritional and herbal treatments for my patients' health problems. My brain is tired of relentless study.

Our condominium faces the Gulf of Mexico. We enjoy daily walks on the barely populated beach. But Maggie doesn't react as I anticipated when she sees the ocean. She goes in, but with much less abandon and enthusiasm compared to last time. I'm saddened by the change. What do I expect, after all? She's going on ten years old. She plays and swims after the ball, but her energy is different. Is maneuvering in the waves painful now? Maybe her arthritis is worse than I thought. It's hard to let in that Maggie has aged.

One morning, mid-trip, my own laughter awakens me from a precious dream:

> *I'm in Madonna's garage and many puppies are leaping into my lap, licking my face. I'm so uplifted by their boundless joy and enthusiasm that I'm laughing a full belly laugh.*

Maggie's wet nose explores my face, bringing me into fuller consciousness. Her eyes are bright, as though she's tickled with my happiness.

"What a joy to hear you wake up this way," Tom is laughing now, too. I realize how easily this deep laughter used to come to me. It's rarer now. *Hmm.*

I walk the beach alone after breakfast. I ponder my life, as I've done so many times before on these shores. Where did my peace of mind go? I feel edgy where I didn't before. Are my changing hormones altering more than my body? Is my profession making me too serious? I've become so cerebral with work, perhaps forcing myself into a way of being that isn't natural for me. I begin to recognize the stirrings of change....

A pelican dives into a wave for its prey, while sandpipers scatter beside me and probe the sand. Serenity and contentment come to me so readily on this island.

I'm reluctant to leave, as usual.

Some of my dreams throughout 2000 may be trying to make me aware—through Maggie—that my life has become too logical and rational in its direction:

- *Maggie is sinking deeply in quicksand with only her head above the sand.*

- *Someone leaves Maggie outside unattended. I see a large, dark heap in the street and am terrified that she was hit by a car.*

- *I leave Maggie tied near the road, where she can wonder into traffic, while I drive off to do something. She's anxious that I am leaving without her, and my heart aches for leaving her there in danger.*

- *I let Maggie out and she's gone longer than usual. I don't go look for her because I'm so busy. I don't know if she got lost, stolen, or hit by a car. It hasn't fully hit me even though it's been two days. When I let it in just for a moment, the pain of not having her and the fact that I didn't look for her is unbearable to let in. I know she isn't coming back now and I'm so sad, but still distracted with other things in my life.*

- *Maggie is heading down a train track into the path of an oncoming train. Tom and I are terrified, screaming for her.*

- *Bobbie (a person I don't feel particularly connected to or trust), puts Maggie in my car for me. A lot of time passes, and I wonder if she left the windows open. I tell myself not to worry, to trust. But the sun is out and it's hot. What if she left her in a closed car? What if Maggie dies in there?*

During my monthly dream-interpretation sessions with Theresa, my Jungian therapist, she teaches me that dream characters often represent an aspect of ourselves. "Dreams are not literal. But they can have more than one meaning." Whatever my dream characters experience is symbolic of me or lessons I need to learn. So am I living "too much in my head" with my body wisdom submerged "in the quicksand"?

And why do I keep having these disturbing dreams about leaving Maggie in danger? Am I too distracted with work to attend properly to her and keep her safe? But I spend *so* much time with her.

I'm not discounting my intellectual, left-brain pursuits. But perhaps I am overdoing it and my imbalance keeps me out of touch with the valuable knowing of intuition. Is Maggie showing me in my dreams that I'm distracted and disconnected from what matters most?

It's early fall of 2000. The results of Maggie's thyroid tests are not making sense to my nurse practitioner brain. The two values measured seem to contradict rather than complement each other. I question Dr. Rupp about the discrepancy quite a bit, but he isn't concerned about it. My enduring questions begin to annoy him. The stress and tension in his bedside manner become more difficult for me to ignore.

My dreams continue:

> *I'm talking to a young couple. Maggie is with me and I tell them how important she is to me—that I can't imagine life without her. He breeds Labradors and gives me his card. He*

wants to give me a puppy when Maggie dies. I think it is a sweet gesture, but I don't want a Lab puppy from a breeder. I want Maggie, and if something happens to her, I want to do Labrador rescue work.

During the period I have these dreams, I don't have a clue that my unconscious is tackling what my conscious mind can't begin to conceive—choices for a future without her—*literal* messages that Maggie is in danger. Had these dreams been grouped together, perhaps their communications would be more obvious. Instead, they are scattered among countless others over time that have nothing to do with Maggie—like messages in a bottle at sea, waiting to be found.

I only later learn that it is possible to have clairvoyant dreams, where we actually perceive something before it happens, perhaps when it's on the verge. Or that we can have prophetic dreams, in which we see the more distant future.[1] These dreams may be delivered in symbolism, but their messages can be quite literal. This is a foreign concept to me, that intuitive information can be received through dreams. I learn that even Carl Jung believed dreams could be prophetic, either about small matters or important events. An emotional charge may come with a prophetic dream that doesn't accompany other types of dreams. Dreams may also be telepathic, where communication occurs with others through means other than the senses.[2]

My dear friend, Judith, recommends Dr. Villano, since I'm uncomfortable with Dr. Rupp's manner and I want another opinion regarding Maggie's thyroid test results. It's November when I stop taking Maggie to Dr. Rupp and make my first acupuncture appointment with Dr. Villano the following week. The room is comfortable, more like a family room than an exam room. Maggie settles on the large area rug with her needles, much more relaxed in this setting. Dr. Villano isn't concerned with her thyroid test results either. So I let my concerns go about her thyroid levels being off and remind myself that my specialty is to diagnose humans, not canines.

There's something vaguely familiar about him—his thin stature, the dark hair and complexion. On the drive home, the light comes on. I saw Dr. Villano once almost ten years ago at the Pet Care 24 Clinic when Maggie was a puppy. I found him to be quite flippant back then. I'm unsettled when I realize this was the same man.

Maybe I misjudged him, I tell myself. After all, that was a long time ago, and Judith really likes him. I like that he's into alternative treatments and that Maggie doesn't have to get onto a table she fears to receive the acupuncture needles. And he is much calmer than Dr. Rupp. Maybe I should give him the benefit of the doubt. I ignore my past sense of him. Unknowingly, I am sacrificing my innate perceptions.

Within days of our first appointment with Dr. Villano, I dream the following:

> *Maggie is losing hair on her chin and neck and getting bald spots. Dr. Villano doesn't really have any suggestions for helping it. Someone else in his office makes a suggestion, but I realize he doesn't know.*

Little do I know how prophetic this dream will become. Unrecognized by her vets, Maggie's thyroid lab tests are indeed off, and she is headed for trouble.

Chapter Twelve
Misdiagnosis and Denial

*M*y twenty-five-year-old nephew, Brad, moves back in with us after completing his geology degree at the University of Montana in early January 2001. He lived with us once before for a couple of months prior to moving to Missoula to attend school. Once again, Tom and I are adjusting to living with a young adult. Poor Brad left his college friends and his girlfriend back in Missoula to look for a job in Denver as a geologist. I'm sure he finds us a far cry from his college roommates. To make matters worse, his relationship with his girlfriend is on the rocks. He's miserable. A great deal of my focus goes to Brad during his difficult time. Our life is a bit chaotic. Maggie falls a bit into the background.

A few days after Brad's arrival, Maggie rolls on her back in our bedroom—her typical morning routine. She groans with pleasure while I rub her belly. That's when I feel it—the strange mass on the right side of her throat. Oh my God! My heart races; my gut tightens. I struggle for a deep breath. It's been two years since her mast cell surgery. Is the cancer back? I sit back in shock.

But later, I *reason* with myself. Of course cancer is the first thing I'd worry about with her history, but maybe it's something else. I calm myself with that thought.

I show Dr. Villano the mass when I take her for her acupuncture appointment a few days later. I also tell him Maggie is panting more than usual for wintertime. She sits patiently as he examines her neck. He isn't at all alarmed by what he feels, which confuses and reassures me at the same time.

"I think Maggie has laryngeal paralysis, a condition common in older Labs with hypothyroidism. You are feeling hypertrophy—increased muscle mass—of her muscles on the paralyzed side of her larynx, because that side has to work harder to open her laryngeal flaps when she breathes. I'm impressed you could feel that," he says.

I'm confused again, since I found it easy to palpate. He goes on to explain that this condition results in a narrowing of the opening of the trachea (windpipe). "Because panting is the only way a dog has to cool herself, it increases to compensate for the narrower airway. She has the *classic* symptoms of laryngeal paralysis."

I never heard of this ailment before. But his explanation makes perfect sense! I'm so relieved he doesn't think it's a tumor. I am surprised, though, since it felt like a nodule to me. *But he is the veterinarian, I'm not,* I rationalize. *Surely he would at least suspect a cancer tumor if there is even a remote chance of one.*

How wrong I am.

He brings up the "unlikely possibility" of a cancer and tells me that the laryngeal area is a "very rare site for cancer in Labradors." He also paints a very grim picture if it is cancer. "The prognosis for cancers in the throat area is very poor, and those surgeries are very difficult and messy. There are so many blood vessels in that area." His voice tone and body language give the impression it would be a horrible ordeal to put Maggie through. The unspoken message I receive is, "You don't want to do that to your dog."

Maggie looks from Dr. Villano and back to me as we speak, as though she is following our conversation.

"I guess we *could* send her for a biopsy," he shrugs his shoulder. His voice sounds hesitant. I read a lack of conviction in his body language and take his uncertainty to mean he doesn't believe a biopsy is necessary.

"What's the point? I won't put her through it if you don't think this is cancer and you're certain it's laryngeal paralysis," I say, "especially if nothing can be done if it *is* cancer."

He nods. "Okay." He continues to write in her chart without making eye contact.

My take-away message? Cancer is unlikely, but if it is, I might as well kiss my dog good-bye. Throat surgery of any kind would be a cruel therapy. I can't even begin to entertain this hopeless possibility. I place my trust in his hands and in his diagnosis. The sinking body feelings I experienced when I first discovered her throat lump went underground—I discount my original intuition.

I leave Dr. Villano's office convinced that my girl has laryngeal paralysis. His presentation invited the cancer concern to leave my mind. A second opinion doesn't even cross my mind. I'm unaware that the hopeless prognosis he painted in the unlikely event of cancer is too painful for me to cope with; it creates a blind spot of denial.

I have a series of disturbing dream fragments within a few weeks of our January visit with Dr. Villano:

- *I have too much thyroid medication ... or am I running out?*

- *Someone gives me a pipe bomb. I try to move away from it in case it explodes. I am waiting for debris to hit me.*

- *A huge tidal wave is coming. The waves are huge, towering, and very close, ready to break over me.*

- *I go through a door. As it closes behind me, I realize I'm stuck in this empty room with no handles on the doors, no way to get out.*

What do these impending-disaster dreams mean? Is the thyroid discrepancy still an issue needing attention?

I continue to take Maggie to Dr. Villano's office monthly for acupuncture to support her overall energy and health. The dreams continue:

- *I am sitting at a table outdoors eating with a group of people. There are busy streets at both ends of the block. Maggie is running around with other dogs. When she comes back to me, I notice there is a big swollen lump on her chest and an abraded area on her side. She has been hit by a car and is hurt! I am devastated. She growls at me when I touch it. I take her to a female vet very close to where we are. She says, "If you can treat them right away, they have a better chance." Now I'm next to Maggie, lying on the side of the road. I know she is in pain; she could be bleeding internally and no one is helping her. I think about trying to carry her but don't know if I can. I feel stuck and helpless.*

- *Tom tells me Maggie was whimpering on her walk. He knows she is in pain and has her euthanized. I am horrified. My heart is breaking. I am in disbelief, grief-stricken.*

- *Maggie and I are driving in a mountain setting. Later, I think she has a headache and I'm going to take her to the vet. Then I notice the right side of her face and neck is red. It's too early for the vet to be open, but I go in to see how soon I can get her in. Dr. Villano is there in a back room, working on a human baby with its belly open and organs exposed. It is breathing, but then I realize it's dead and the breathing is simulated. He says this is how he practices where to give shots to animals. I'm appalled and repulsed by what he is doing, by his unethical way of practicing.*

Why am I dreaming we are euthanizing Maggie? That Dr. Villano is practicing inappropriately?

The palpable lump disappears and Maggie's throat is symmetrical again. But her throat feels firmer and larger to me. I think this is the increasing hypertrophy secondary to her overworked muscles from worsening laryngeal paralysis described by Dr. Villano; she may be developing it on the *other* side. Dr. Villano never checks Maggie's neck again between January and May. I guess he isn't concerned.

As the weather warms, Maggie's panting increases with even slight exertion or excitement. Dr. Villano tells me this is expected with laryngeal paralysis; my Internet research confirms it. Tom, Maggie, and I spend Easter Sunday at Tom's sister's house. Lou expresses concern that Maggie is stressed. Had we become so accustomed to the gradual increase of her panting? My stomach churns. I ache as I let in the pace and intensity of it. I can't bear the thought of Maggie's increasing discomfort. I hadn't realized how adversely laryngeal paralysis could affect her. Doubt is creeping in about her diagnosis.

We are leaving the next day for a sailing trip in the Caribbean for two weeks. We leave our family gathering early and take Maggie to Pet Care 24 Clinic that day. Dr. Gordon is not working, so we see Dr. Banks, who we haven't met before. The clinic is very reputable; we have every reason to trust them from our past experiences there.

"Feel her throat," I direct her. "It feels hard. It just doesn't feel right to me. Could it be a tumor?" I am glad to be getting a second opinion. Have I been deluding myself?

Once again, Maggie sits on the stainless steel exam table in her compliant manner and allows the woman to palpate her neck. She licks her arm.

"She is an older dog, and her neck muscles are somewhat *atrophied.* That makes her throat structures more prominent, which is what you are feeling. It's not uncommon for older dogs to have decreased muscle mass compared to younger dogs," she explains.

Hmm. Atrophied muscles are the *opposite* of hypertrophied (larger) muscles that Dr. Villano described.

Dr. Banks takes a chest x-ray to view Maggie's heart and lungs. "Her heart and lungs look great. Her laryngeal area is included in the film, although the actual structures won't show on an x-ray. Cancer is always something to consider, but there are no shadows around the larynx that indicate a tumor there. Cancer is not what I suspect. I, too, think you are looking at a classic case of laryngeal paralysis."

She gives us good management tips for the ailment. "Keep her food and water bowl elevated to make swallowing easier; choking will be less likely, also. Be sure to keep her cool so she won't have to pant so hard to cool herself." Dr. Villano hadn't mentioned the feeding aids; we are grateful, since we appreciate *anything* we can do to support Maggie's comfort.

As with Dr. Villano, Dr. Banks doesn't recommend a biopsy or follow-up, either. Relieved and reassured, we go home to finish our packing.

Tom and I leave the next day for our sailing trip with friends to the Grenadine Islands and leave our animals in Brad's hands. Our first sailboat experience is unique and lovely, yet I am distracted the entire time. Unsettled. I always missed Maggie when we traveled. Still, I found it easy to immerse myself in the beauty, new experiences, and people that travel offered. Not this time. I am unable to get her off my mind. I can't wait until we moor at an island with a telephone so I can call to check on her. I'm *obsessed* with getting back to her. Given the churning in my gut, my body isn't convinced by the reassurances from either vet regarding Maggie.

"All is well," Brad reports with each call. "Maggie is just

fine."

I'm so relieved after each call. Then my body goes back into subtle fight-or-flight as the anxiety creeps back in. I just want to go home and be with her.

All is *not* well. On some level, I know that. I always look forward to returning home to her, but this extreme vigilance is not my norm. I researched enough about laryngeal paralysis to know that if it threatens her ability to breathe, the treatment is a tracheotomy (an incision to create a permanent hole in her airway to allow air to enter her lungs). That will mean the end of swimming, which Maggie lives for. I can't bear the thought of making that decision. But Dr. Villano thinks hers is a *mild* case.

Then why is her panting so intense, even in cool weather? Why does she tire so easily on our hikes?

The day arrives at last. We drive into our garage, and I can't jump out of the car fast enough. I burst into the family room. Maggie greets us at the door with her usual exuberance.

"Oh, you're home! You're home!" her face shouts as she leaps and turns happy circles; she washes our faces with her tongue. I am where I belong. I settle inside.

Dr. Villano's partner, Dr. Crystal, sees Maggie for her May acupuncture since Dr. Villano is out of town. I haven't met her before and like her a lot. Maggie slides her body against Dr. Crystal and looks at her sideways in her coquettish way, the whites of her eyes showing ever so slightly. She raises her paw and places it on Dr. Crystal's lap. I think Maggie approves of her new health care person. Do I read concern in Dr. Crystal's face as she examines my girl?

Three weeks pass. It's late May, time for spring planting. I want to finish before my mom and dad arrive in a few days. I started growing my red salvia and impatiens seedlings indoors under grow lights in March. I nursed them along once again; they look better than ever—leaves are a rich green and buds are already opening. I'm so proud. Maggie joins me in the yard in our yearly planting ritual, tying into the raw soup bone I give her. Her tail thumps on the ground when I speak to her or walk by, but she is too engrossed in her bone to look up.

A freak snowstorm hits. My tender annuals, having been in the ground for only a week, are reduced to stems sticking out of the dirt. I cry at the loss of my long-nurtured creation. I can't bring myself to pull them up and replant. I want my flowers that I put so much time and love into growing. I refuse to go buy greenhouse plants—for now. In defiance, I leave the pitiful stubs in the ground. Maybe they'll rally. A comforting thought.

I leave my practice at the women's clinic since I want to try my hand at writing. I wrestled with this decision for months. It's a major transition, yet when I finally act, it's a tiny bleep on the radar screen amidst Brad's turmoil, my parents' visit, and Maggie's worrisome symptoms.

I'm already querying publishers of health magazines. Writing health-related articles seems a safe and logical step, given my background; plus, I was published in three nursing journals several years ago.

Soon, tiny green buds appear on the red salvia stems. True to their name, the impatiens plants take their time. Within a few weeks, though, they, too, are making a comeback. As I observe the death and gradual rebirth of my flowers, my angel's breathing becomes increasingly labored in sleep.

This is getting bad, I admit to myself. It's *not mild* laryngeal paralysis. I fear she'll soon need that tracheotomy. Of course, jumping into a lake would mean drowning. How can I condone a lifesaving measure that will deny Maggie her greatest pleasure?

We are having new siding put on our house that spring. Most

years, the tree swallows nest in a hole the woodpeckers kindly bore through our house just under our roof line. I warn Randy, the contractor, that there are likely to be baby birds nestled into those holes. I ask him to please listen and peer into all holes before he seals them over with new siding.

Sure enough, when Maggie and I return home this early June afternoon, Randy comes from the back of the house to meet us in the driveway with a small cardboard box. I look in to see five almost featherless babies. Maggie stares up at the box with her inquisitive, nurturing eyes, while her tail wags in hopeful anticipation that she may initiate tactile exploration with her nose.

I know Maggie will not harm the babies. Randy, however, does not have the faith that my Labrador's bird hunting genes will lie dormant. His eyes grow large and his mouth drops as I hold the box under Maggie's nose for a sniff. Her face has a sweet, caring look. Randy finds her gentleness in this circumstance incredulous.

I race to the phone with Mags on my heels. Cinnamon greets Maggie and me at the front door and rises up on her hind legs like a squirrel to sniff around Maggie's mouth—very cute—a strange new behavior over the last couple of months.

After I speak with Greenwood Wildlife Sanctuary, I grab a Tupperware bowl from the kitchen. Following their advice, I ask Randy to screw it into the tree as close as possible to the original nest, as Greenwood directed. I look up from the base of the tree, grateful for the length of his ladder. Maggie observes Randy as he places a ragged aqua tarp from the bed of his pickup to protect the defenseless babies from the sun, high enough above the nest for mama and papa swallow to fly under.

The pair of swallows *finally* tends to the nest after we watch and fret for several long hours.

Two days later, Maggie is having her acupuncture with Dr. Crystal again. Her brow furrows into unmistakable concern.

"Maggie's neck feels odd. Something is not right."

I agree, but since two vets already evaluated Maggie's neck for a tumor and her x-rays were negative, I'm not slightly concerned about cancer at this point. Dr. Crystal requests that I have Maggie's April x-rays sent to her.

Wow, do I have my head buried in the sand.

The summer is passing quickly, as they always seem to. At the end of June, I dream:

> *Maggie is lying in the backseat of the car. Suddenly, she stops breathing and dies. I don't try to shake her into breathing. Later, I wish I had. I am crushed. I walk around our house outside; when I come back to the front yard, I see Maggie lying still in the weeds across the street. I keep hoping she will wake up and start breathing. I don't want to quit hoping....*

I wake up crying, with my heart pounding.

It's a hot summer. I begin awakening during the night. Although my changing hormones have played havoc with my sleep for some time now, this is different. There sits my baby love—panting—obviously in some distress. Do I feel it in my sleep? She seems more comfortable sitting rather than lying down. I get up, drench towels in cold water, and place them on her heaving body to cool her. Maggie licks and nibbles my chin; her eyes glow with gratitude and find mine. We connect—the synergy of our love pours from her eyes to mine and back—into my soul. Does she feel it too, in the depths of her being? Then she lies back down with a sigh, rests her head on her paws, and is calm at last. At least for the moment. Sleep finally comes to my angel.

Daytime is a different story. After a sluggish morning, Maggie is herself—energetic and eager to swim. Next, she delights in riding into town, greets people (as is her norm), and charms anyone she can out of a dog treat. When we return home, she charges into our bedroom, grabs her favorite squeaky sheepskin "dolly," and engages me in a quick game of fetch. Back and forth she gallops. She makes deceiving myself easy.

Yet I do sense a change in Maggie's energy. She rests much longer in the morning before she gets going. I seem to filter out that her unique mannerisms occur less often. I don't consider that perhaps the enthusiasm she musters is for *our* benefit.

I've been craving a retreat for quite awhile. Just for a couple of days. I love being married, yet I miss the solitude that came so easy when I was single; I need to indulge it now and then. I enjoy camping and thrive in nature. Tom, Maggie, and I scout for my camping spot. I decide on Rainbow Lakes, forty-five minutes from home. It's perfect. I drive up to my spot on Monday, July 2, to beat the July Fourth crowds. I don't take Maggie, since I plan two long hikes and there are no streams along the trails for her to cool off in. She can't hike that far anymore, which I've adapted to. There is only one other person camping almost a mile away. It's a rare treat to have such privacy without going into the back country. I spend two glorious nights in the arms of the forest.

After I replenish my soul in the woods, I'm eager to head home to Tom, Maggie, and Cinnamon on the morning of July fourth. What a peaceful drive along the Peak-to-Peak highway. A stunning Colorado summer morning. Bright sunshine. Clear blue skies. I wind my way through the outdated town of Ward—reminiscent of an auto junkyard, but still quaint—down Left Hand Canyon toward home.

As I approach the lake in our subdivision, I'm happy to see Tom's car parked at the beach. Time for Maggie's daily swim and fetch. I park my car and get out. I catch Maggie's glimpse of recognition from the shoreline, where she stands dripping wet, ball in mouth. Her focus on me is intent. Velvet ears perk. Her tail begins a slow sway, then increases in speed. No longer able to contain herself, Maggie bolts toward me like an excited puppy. My heart melts and overflows with love for her. Upon reaching me, her feet leave the ground when she leaps into the air. Her face exudes joy. I am astounded at the gusto she displays, since she is far from a youngster now. Our eyes meet. As do our hearts. Love fills me. I know she feels it, too. If I could capture ecstasy in a dog, this surely is it. I know this priceless, touching moment will be etched in my being for the rest of my life. What an honor to be so loved. To receive such a beautiful welcome! The way a small child responds to a parent—until peers become everything and to show affection is no longer in vogue. What a gift this moment is.

"Now you know why I have such a deep connection with her," I hug Tom. "Who else in the world greets me with such pure joy and ecstasy?" I wink at him. He's a close second with the way his face illuminates in welcome. Maggie's loyalty and unbridled love for me, the way she lights up *whenever* I show up, allows me to experience an adoration I haven't known before—one of the unique beauties canines offer their humans. Parents are the foundation their children develop and create their own lives from, but parents lose center stage as a child explores further outward—as it should be. Not so with canines' parents. We are always worth their love and devotion.

Chapter Thirteen
The Painful Truth

"**W**as Maggie ever hit by a car?" Dr. Crystal asks. It's Monday, July 9, when she reviews Maggie's April x-rays with me.

"What? No!" I am confused. "Why?"

"Her sternum was broken at some point in her life. It's totally healed now, but it was definitely broken."

I am stunned. The vet at the 24-hour clinic didn't mention this at all when she reviewed Maggie's chest x-ray in April. How could she have broken her sternum and exhibited no signs of pain or any change in activity? Is that what set her up for such early arthritis?

Thoughts race through my head. Had something happened to her with our house sitter when we were away on one of our trips? Did something happen during her mast cell surgery that we weren't informed of? I can't imagine.

Dr. Crystal expresses concern about how Maggie's neck *feels*. As the vet at Pet Care 24 Clinic *saw* nothing unusual on the x-ray, neither did Dr. Crystal.

She asks Dr. Villano to come feel Maggie's throat, since he felt it initially. The pained look of concern and compassion on Dr. Villano's face as he palpates Maggie's neck tells me the horrible truth.

"I think you need to have her neck cut open to do a biopsy," he advises. I sit there in shock. "I don't know what this is, but something is very wrong. It feels symmetrical, which is good, since cancer is typically asymmetrical. It may be some kind of sclerosing disease, which can't be good either."

I am paralyzed. "No! You can't be telling me this now!" my mind screams. "Not six months later!" My heart sinks. My lungs hunger for air. What my body had known surfaces, and the confusion between my body and conscious mind clears and becomes congruent.

Why hadn't Dr. Villano checked her throat since January? He was obviously convinced it wasn't a tumor. His lack of concern about cancer over the four months he saw Maggie and the two expert opinions persuaded me: Maggie's throat changes were due to muscle changes from laryngeal paralysis.

"We can try a course of antibiotics in the off-chance it's an infection," he offers. I know he doesn't believe it is. Nor do I. I *know* now it *is* cancer. Desperate, I take them. I drive home in a daze.

The agonizing truth crashes over me. I had overridden my own intuition with expert opinions. I lived in denial by ignoring what my fingers told me back in January. After the second opinion, I accepted that Maggie's strange, firm throat was part of laryngeal paralysis. I disregarded the way I withdrew my hands from her throat when I toweled her off after her swim—it became foreign and confusing to me. Coming out of my unconscious fog of denial, I realize now that the message my hands gave me conflicted with what the vets told me. *Oh God, I sold out on my own body signals, my own perception—out of fear—I let this progress! I allowed my head—and scientific expertise—to overrule my instinct.*

My dream following my first appointment with Dr. Villano *had been* prophetic. Dr. Villano did *not* know what was wrong with Maggie. Dr. Crystal is the one who discovered the actual, more serious problem—*the other person in his office my dream said would have a suggestion.*

We stop at the lake for Maggie to swim. And for me to try to grasp that I am losing my best friend. How can she seem normal as she swims out and retrieves her ball? Is she changing so gradually I just don't notice? Perhaps I have been looking through a selective lens that only focuses on the Maggie mannerisms and energy I want to see. So I don't have to let in the pain. Maggie is showing me what I later learn—that by the time our animals *act* sick, their illness is often very advanced. This is why cancer is often missed in the early stages. By the time our pets stop doing their usual activities, cancer may be extensive.

I look down at her rolling carefree on her back in the grass. Who would know, looking at her now, that she is dying?

When I get home, I call to make an appointment for Friday with Dr. Gordon at Pet Care 24. That is the soonest I can get in with her; I don't want to see anyone else at this point.

I take Tom in my arms when he gets home from work and tell him. He stares at me in dismay, his face ashen. Our dinner sits on the table untouched.

My niece, Heather, is arriving tomorrow, Tuesday, to stay until Friday afternoon. I am in such distress and in no mood for company, even my niece whom I love dearly.

But I do the best I can. On Wednesday, Heather and I take Maggie up to Diamond Lake, a lovely wildflower hike below Arapaho Pass in the Indian Peaks Wilderness. Maggie is her cute, silly self after dipping in the lake and streams. She runs with abandon up and down the trail and leaps into the air next to us as she flies by. Her face is bright and happy. My God, they really do live fully until their last breath. Maybe Maggie senses my pain—she knows how vital her comfort and happiness are to me—and tries to please me by acting normal.

"Are you sure it's so dismal?" Heather inquires. "Look at her! She's having a great time and seems so normal."

"I know. It's hard to believe, watching her. I keep thinking this is a nightmare I'll wake up from." I am trying to stay out of my dark feelings during Heather's brief visit. I want to make the most of our time together, but in truth, I'm dying inside.

On Friday at Pet Care 24 Clinic, Dr. Gordon's face is grim. She is fairly certain it's cancer. She refers us to Dr. Wausau, a renowned veterinary oncologist at Colorado State University (CSU), a well-respected veterinary school in Fort Collins. We can't get an appointment with him for three days. In the meantime, Dr. Gordon starts Maggie on prednisone to slow the growth of the suspected tumor.

"The tumor growth will slowly block her trachea, making her breathing much more difficult. If her breathing becomes more labored before your appointment, take her to the CSU emergency department immediately," Dr. Gordon instructs.

Maggie follows me up to my office around 9:30 PM and lies down. I watch her breathing. Her chest muscles are working hard, pulling more deeply inward with each breath. This is new, and I'm scared. We rush her to the CSU emergency department around 10:00 PM. The vet student who admits Maggie is so compassionate with us; she falls in love with our girl. She conducts a full examination and draws blood for lab work. Maggie nuzzles the young woman's hand and peers into her face. She seems to know the young vet in training wants to help her. Out comes her washrag tongue as she bathes the student's hand and arm.

"She is just *so* sweet," she remarks. "Maggie is clearly in some distress. We'll need to keep her in our ICU on oxygen to monitor her until Dr. Wausau can do a neck biopsy on Monday."

The student leads us to the ICU so we can see where Maggie will be. It reminds me of my years in neonatal ICU—very high tech. To leave my baby in a small enclosure with an oxygen tube taped to her nose is excruciating, as is the bewildered expression on her face as we walk away without her.

"You can come visit her and take her outside with you for short periods," a veterinary technician tries to reassure us. I'm sure she senses our gut-wrenching agony. I feel so guilty leaving Maggie at such a critical time. I want to comfort her. Spend every moment with her. How can she possibly understand why we are putting her in a cage and leaving without her?

It's all so surreal. This can't be happening to us. Tom and I stay in a motel in Fort Collins. Morning dawns and I awaken. The wall of dreadfulness strikes me head-on. We dress in silence, grab a quick bite, and hurry to CSU. We spend a good part of the day with Maggie, taking her in and out of the ICU. But she is in her own world. We can't connect with her. Is she mad at us for leaving her? Confused? Unfortunately, prednisone can be the culprit that's causing the distance.

Our sweet dog clearly doesn't understand when she is led away from us back into the ICU. She looks back at us through the door longingly as if to say, "*Why* aren't I going with you?" Her eyes no longer sparkle—her entire face emits sadness and resignation. Her tail hangs, as does her head.

Sunday is pretty much a repeat of Saturday. Tom and I say very little during our meals out in Fort Collins. Our hearts are in pieces.

On Monday they shave Maggie's neck and complete the biopsy. As we wait, I hope and pray that by some miracle it isn't cancer and that it's operable if it is.

We receive the devastating news that afternoon: advanced thyroid cancer. Inoperable. A totally different type of cancer than her mast cell cancer—there's no relationship between the two. The oncologist won't touch her surgically at this point. Tumor removal is impossible since the cancer is now embedded in and around Maggie's surrounding throat tissues and blood vessels. Oh my God, it's too late!

The final test is a radioactive scan to see if Maggie's thyroid cancer metastasized anywhere else in her body. I'm not sure why they bother with this test. Perhaps they want to see if she is a candidate for radiation therapy. We are so disappointed when the staff informs us we have to leave her one more night in the ICU so the radioactive dye can pass through her kidneys. Every moment with her counts; leaving her here alone is killing me. We drive back home to stay tonight.

I get on my computer and run a search on thyroid cancer. With searing pain, I discover that Maggie fell outside of the statistics for canine throat cancers that Dr. Villano referred to. To twist the knife deeper, I learn that surgery can be *curative* when thyroid cancer in dogs is caught *early* in the nodular stage. Long-term tumor control has been achieved with small, freely moveable tumors that are completely removed at surgery.[1] One study showed dogs with this type of thyroid tumor and no evidence of metastasis that were treated with surgery alone had a median survival of more than three years.[2] I am devastated. I feel responsible; that I let Maggie down. Sleep does not come easily.

We are in the car on our way to CSU as soon as we get up, dress, and eat a bowl of cereal. We are eager to bring Maggie home. My legs nearly buckle when we learn the results of Maggie's radioactive scan—it shows no cancer *anywhere* else in her body. This makes her dismal prognosis an even greater torture. I blame myself—feel tremendous guilt—for not taking her to CSU myself for a biopsy back in January when the cancer was merely a small nodule. But I'm at a loss as to why Dr. Villano didn't refer us to CSU when it's practically in our backyard—didn't *insist* that Maggie have a biopsy. I feel robbed of precious time that could have been ours.

CSU offers radiation therapy for the thyroid cancer. They say it can shrink the tumor and perhaps give her another year to eighteen months. I would drive her the hour each way to CSU every day for six weeks. She'd be there for a couple of hours. Maggie's throat structures would be damaged from the radiation. It would burn and cause her pain. She'd have difficulty swallowing. She may not want to eat. It would heal in a few months. Maybe, just maybe, if we could be reassured that she wouldn't have a recurrence soon afterward. Of course, we couldn't be.

It's a no-brainer for Tom and me. Not for our full-of-life girl. We don't want a good part of her last days spent in a veterinary hospital with *any* added discomfort to what she already has. We'll make her life as normal, fun, and comfortable as we can. For as long as possible. Until she stops smiling. Our girl will go out as close to still having her dancing shoes on as possible.

Yet people go through radiation therapy and chemotherapy all the time for cancer. They allow their quality of life to be interfered with either temporarily or for the remainder of their lives. Why is it different for our dog? Perhaps because human adults can make their *own* decisions. Parents make the decision for their children, but they can *explain* to their children what's going on. Children can tell their parents when they've had enough and are ready to go. Our animals are at our mercy because they can't speak for themselves.

Maggie bursts through the door leading from the ICU when the vet technician brings her to us in the waiting room. Heads turn at her lively entry. She jumps up on the business office counter to peer in and let the woman know that she is aware there are treats up there. And yes, she would like one, thank you. Even in our heartsick state, we can't help but smile.

Maggie's shaven neck becomes irritated and red. Each night, I apply cream to soothe the irritation and gently wipe her bald neck with a cold, damp washcloth. In a haze, I think back to last November, to the thyroid tests with Dr. Rupp that didn't make sense to me and the dream fragment that questioned whether I have *too much or too little thyroid medication.* Slowly, it begins to dawn on me that I saw her neck like this before. In my dreams, months ago: *Maggie is losing hair on her chin and neck—getting bald spots. Her face and neck are red.* How is it possible that my dreams predicted this months in advance? Five months before Maggie is diagnosed with thyroid cancer, the information was delivered to my unconscious. Within one month after I discovered the lump. When it was early and probably still operable.

I don't understand it. I also can't ignore it.

We know Maggie's days are numbered, so we try to make the most of them. It feels like providence that Tom has two weeks scheduled off work during this time for our yearly July Crested Butte trip. Of course, that trip is out of the question. We take day trips with Maggie to Estes Park, Barker Reservoir in Nederland, and of course, McGuckin's and the Brewing Market. We think we are trying to make her days as normal and alive as possible. Perhaps it is we who need the sense of normalcy.

Tom spends the morning with her at the St.Vrain River in Jamestown while I stay home to research alternative cancer therapies on the Internet. I have to feel I'm leaving no stone unturned. I think my immersion into research to find a way to heal Maggie's cancer is the only control I can feel in this out-of-control situation. It's easier than dealing with my agonizing emotions.

With the thyroid cancer growing and pressing on her larynx, the quality of Maggie's bark weakens, as they predicted within days of her return from CSU. That evening, Tom and I are eating dinner on our bedroom deck. Maggie sits in her spot at our sides, waiting for her inevitable after-dinner morsels.

"I haven't heard her bark today, have you?" I ask Tom with sadness.

He shakes his head—his face grim.

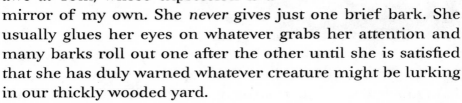

To our utter amazement, without missing a beat, Maggie looks away from us out toward our yard, does a nervous little trot, and gives one short bark. It seems urgent. In direct response to what I said. Her eyes immediately focus back on ours—her face intent—as if to say, "Yes, I can still do it."

Chills travel my spine. I look in awe at Tom, whose expression is a mirror of my own. She *never* gives just one brief bark. She usually glues her eyes on whatever grabs her attention and many barks roll out one after the other until she is satisfied that she has duly warned whatever creature might be lurking in our thickly wooded yard.

I think this is one of Maggie's parting gifts. It feels like it is important to her that she let us know before she leaves, *"Yes, I do understand what you say. I do tune into your thoughts. I know so much more than you realize."*

We are walking a fine line—to not deny Maggie life while she still has quality—and to not wait too long. The tumor could grow large enough to suffocate her. Although her light is dimming, Maggie still seems to enjoy going places, seeing people, getting out for a short walk, and hanging her head out the car window. She still eats with gusto.

"How will we know when it's time?" I ask a friend who has been there. The thought of actually letting go is excruciating.

"You'll know," she encourages. "Just trust yourself. She'll let you know."

I didn't ask to play God. I don't like or want the role.

The prednisone is supposed to offer Maggie a sense of well-being in addition to slowing the tumor growth. It also alters her personality; she is somewhat removed. Yet she still has moments of presence and enthusiasm. Her anxiety is growing ever-so-slightly each day, but it's difficult to know if it is due to a side effect of the prednisone or to inadequate oxygenation. Her appetite increases—another side effect of the prednisone. She is eating more but starting to lose weight; cancer metabolism has begun.

I speak with a very well-respected chiropractor in Boulder, noted for his use of nutritional therapies with cancer patients. I am touched when he returns my call on a Sunday afternoon after being out of town. People often wait months to see him.

I won't ever forget his compassion. In his gentle, empathetic manner he offers little hope. He helps me accept that we did all we could. There is nothing left to do. He facilitates me in beginning to let go. It's actually a relief to cease my attempts to try to save Maggie, because it is taking me away from simply *being* with her.

Chapter Fourteen
The Magic Is Gone

*I*t is Monday, July 23, 2001. Maggie's countenance starts to droop. We take her to the park at Boulder Creek, hoping it will perk her up. It doesn't. Next, we try the Brewing Market. She exhibits minimal interest in interacting with people. We take her to lunch with us at Qdoba; Maggie loses her balance while urinating in the grass there. With all the pressure on her neck, I consider for the first time that she may have a bad headache. Tormented, we go home. Maggie follows  my every move throughout the house. She's been glued to me this past week and is even more so today.

Late that afternoon, I decide to go for a drive alone. She trails me to the door; her eyes plead to go with me. I sense she is deriving her energy to live from me somehow. I feel drained. By this time, I am bargaining with the powers-that-be. According to Elizabeth Kubler-Ross, bargaining is one of the stages we go through during the dying process.[1] Have I become *too* connected to Maggie, perhaps in an unhealthy way? Maybe if I can just demonstrate that I can leave without her, she won't die. Of course it doesn't make sense—so much doesn't make sense when we are losing a beloved pet or person in our lives.

As I drive through the country, I experience the painful loneliness of no longer having her with me, and I know this is merely the tiniest tip of the iceberg. No warm pink tongue to lick my hand when I reach back to her. No deep brown eyes study me from the backseat.

I'm not gone for long. I see the anguish that's taken up residence in Tom's face as he and Maggie watch me climb up the stairs.

"This is so intense. I need a break from all of this," he says. "I'm going to a movie this evening for a little escape."

I appreciate the alone time with Maggie. We haven't had that for awhile. I sit next to her in the living room and gently run my hand over her body. "Just let me know when it's time, baby girl." She gets up, moves away from me, and finds another spot to lie. I'm sad she doesn't want me to comfort her, helpless. I can see her retractions with each breath, a pulling in of her chest muscles as she labors at what was once so natural. She doesn't lie for long.

I walk out to the deck to do flower maintenance—to distract myself—it's hard to sit still. Maggie follows, panting heavily. She wants to be in my proximity but doesn't want me to touch or talk to her. She begins to pace. It dawns on me that she is more anxious. The reality hits hard. *She is letting me know.* It strikes me that she may experience more pressure on her trachea (airway) when lying rather than standing. Oh God, she can't get enough air lying down! I feel nauseated. This is it. We both know it.

It's getting dark when I get into the shower. Maybe the warm water will relax me. My head is spinning. Should we go as soon as Tom gets home? What if I'm wrong? Maybe I should cut back on the prednisone and see if it helps, in case that's causing the anxiety....

Tom walks in a little after 10:00 PM. I take his hands and gaze intently in his eyes. "Honey, it's time," I whisper.

"No! Not yet. It can't be! I'm not ready." He thought we'd have more than a week with her—that the prednisone would buy us more time. So did I.

I am so keyed-in to Maggie's energy. Knowing it's time, I can't be in her presence and sleep. I feel like I am betraying her. I'm so torn. But I owe it to Tom to come to his own readiness as I have.

"I'll wait, but I can't sleep in the same room with her." I can't bear it, waiting when I believe it's time. But it also lets me hold on just a little longer. Tom takes Maggie to sleep near him in the downstairs guest room.

It doesn't take him long. At 2:00 AM, Tom awakens me. "It's time, Honey. Maggie woke me up. She is *so* anxious. She's having difficulty breathing."

His voice is shaking. We hold each other tightly for a moment—both of us wanting desperately to awaken from this dreadful nightmare.

I run to the downstairs bedroom, where Maggie sits panting, her face worried. There is no question. "Come on, baby love. Let's go," I can barely hear my voice. She follows me up the stairs, where I quickly change clothes. Cinnamon sits a few feet away, watching Maggie. Tom calls Pet Care 24 Clinic and explains the situation. They tell us to bring her in; they will prepare for her.

"Say good-bye to your friend," I tell Cinnamon through my tears. "She is really struggling and we have to help her leave now." Cinnamon continues taking it all in, saunters over, and rubs against Maggie in the way she marks what's hers. Maggie licks the top of Cinnamon's head once; then we walk out of our room, down the hallway, and head down to the front door.

The three of us walk outside to the Blazer parked in the driveway. Maggie hesitates to glance back at our house and around the yard before she steps into the car. I sense she knows she is leaving home for the last time, and she drinks it in. She sticks her head out the car window for several minutes, the way she loves to, before she curls up and lays down. I attempt to move her next to me. She resists and stays in her own space instead. When Shanna was so sick just before we had her euthanized, she disappeared in the house and hid behind our hanging robes. I have heard that animals in nature go off to themselves when it's time to die. Maggie seems to be doing her own version of that. Tom and I drive in silence, with reality suspended.

When we get to the clinic, I direct Maggie onto the scale, which she usually does with ease. She glances at me as if to say, "You're kidding, right? What does it matter?" For some inexplicable reason, I want to know how much weight she lost. Five pounds.

Maggie wags her tail at the vet—another new face—and the vet technician. "Do you want to stay with her during the euthanasia?" the veterinarian asks.

"Oh, of course," we both nod. I can't imagine not being at her side at her journey's end. I know for others it might be too unbearable to be present at their pets' euthanasia, just like some of us prefer not to be present at the death of a loved family member. There is no right or wrong way to do it.

It seems impossible not to question whether we are doing it too soon or waiting too long when any of us are faced with this decision to put our beloved pets "to sleep." We often second-guess ourselves no matter when we do it.

Her name is Dr. Bates. She leads all of us into an exam

room. There is a large blanket on the floor and a pink syringe on the counter. Maggie, panting heavily, takes every treat offered to her as she paces back and forth in the small room. "I see what you mean about her anxiety," Dr. Bates says. "Do you want some time alone with her first?"

"No, let's just do it," we both say in unison. It is unbearable for us to watch Maggie—feeling now that she *is* suffering—that we may have waited too long. We are nervous and want to get it over with for her sake.

"Okay. Go ahead and call her over to you onto the blanket."

Tom and I sit near the blanket. I'm minimally aware of the bright lights and my slight irritation at the vet technicians' presence. Rather than carrying out a necessary function, she seems to be purely observing. Only later does it occur to me that I wish I had asked her to dim the lights, then to please leave. We didn't know the vet could have given Maggie a sedative first. That might have calmed her down *and* given us precious time with her to say good-bye.

"Come here, baby girl," I whisper gently to Maggie as I pat the blanket. Then she does something Tom and I will never forget. She walks over and stands with her head in a corner and her back to us. It feels like she is saying, "No! I don't want to say good-bye to you!" We don't understand what it means or why she does it, but it rips our hearts into shreds. It will haunt me years into the future whenever I think of it.

"Come on, baby." Tears stream down my face as I get up and place my hands gently on each side of her. "Come on, honey." She turns, walks with resignation to the blanket, and lies down. I sit behind her and cradle my arms around her; Tom sits at her head. Dr. Bates places the tourniquet over Maggie's leg and finds her vein. She isn't even halfway through the injection when Maggie gasps deeply. Her body totally relaxes as she slowly slumps back into my lap and arms.

At approximately 3:00 AM on July 24, 2001, my canine soul

mate takes her last breath in my arms. Our lives are forever changed. The *Magic* is indeed gone.

My mind floats back to my girl's amazing Fourth of July greeting. I couldn't have begun to imagine at that moment that in less than three weeks, Maggie would be dead.

Chapter Fifteen
Intuition Never Lies

Several weeks after Maggie's death, I review my dream journal. Sometimes I recorded three or four dreams in one night. Theresa and I discussed merely a sampling of my prolific dreams in our monthly sessions. So it was easy to miss the repetitive themes relating to Maggie that I now know were *literally* about her, not just about me. As an apprentice learning about Jungian dream interpretation, I placed a lot of emphasis on Theresa's interpretations. Now that I realize some of my dream messages about Maggie manifested in waking reality, I am motivated to search for more information regarding dream communications.

I buy *Dreams Are Messages from the Soul* by Connie Kaplan. I am spellbound as I read about clairvoyant and prophetic dreams. I glance back at my journal. There it is. The predictions of our impending good-bye are interspersed over seventeen months. As I read through my dreams again—all at one time with this new knowledge—I am powerfully impacted by their premonitory warnings. It's too late to reap information for Maggie, but it is another means to cultivate my inner spiritual messages—a communication channel beyond my logical understanding. Might I have changed Maggie's future if I had recognized this prophetic information ahead of time? That question will remain.

Perhaps my most telltale dream in all of 2000 was this:

I'm waiting for the end of something. I have a sense of impending doom. I try to get Maggie to walk with me, but she won't because she knows we're going to be separated for a long time; she doesn't want that to happen. I don't either, but I'm more resigned to it. I'm not sure why we're being separated. I think we can try to climb this mountain, to hide out from whoever will come for us. I'm not sure who is coming after us or why, but it's inevitable.

Death was the inevitable coming after us, so much sooner than I imagined. Looking back now, my dreams are so clear....

Where did my prophetic dream information come from? That deep place where our two souls merged in sleep? From elsewhere in the spiritual realm? This experience is opening my mind to psychic dreams and information—that it doesn't just come through psychics—that it can come through me, too. I can't absolutely know if a dream is prophetic until the event shows up in waking life, but I will be more discerning with them now. I am particularly attending to the body feelings I have when I wake up from dreams.

In *Beyond Words: Talking with Animals and Nature,* Marta Williams says we are born with the inherent ability to communicate with animals and nature mentally through thoughts, images, and emotions. She believes this is an ancient inborn trait of all life forms.[1] Perhaps my dreams were a medium for Maggie and me to communicate. I used to think psychic phenomenon was reserved for psychics like John Edward or Allison Dubois. I'm beginning to believe that psychic information is available to *all* of us, if we pay attention.

It's been one of my life's major journeys to learn to trust my intuition and body messages. I *believed* in trusting gut over intellect, but I didn't *live* it. I'm not sure I knew how to. I wasn't raised to honor and respect my inner knowing. Years of Catholic schools and upbringing oriented me to an external frame of reference. I learned to continually tune into my parents, mainly my mom, in an attempt to keep my emotional well-being from harm. I danced to their tune to please them. To respond instinctively was sometimes dangerous to my psyche.

With my childhood history and living in a very cerebral culture, I learned to let my head overrule my gut sense, to figure out what others expected of me rather than to search within. To believe expert opinion over my own was not a stretch—when we're distanced from our own inner knowledge, we tend to look outward for answers. Our modern, logic-based society conditions us to suppress our intuitive abilities, but we can get them back if we train ourselves.[2]

I came far in recovering and trusting my inner self before Maggie's illness, but the tendency to fall back into old patterns hadn't completely disappeared, especially under stress. Maggie's life, illness, and untimely death led me to more profoundly honor and nurture my inner world—to respond more from my *internal* frame of reference—to dance to my own tune. In short, Maggie showed me my way *home:* to my heart, my intuition, and to a fuller self-love.

I glimpse at my journal again and reread from months earlier: *Maggie is hurt and no one is helping her ... If you can treat them right away, they have a better chance ...*

A biopsy at that first crucial appointment might have saved her life and given Maggie three more quality years. Still perplexed that he didn't emphasize a biopsy, I write a letter to Dr. Villano. I ask him why he didn't refer us to the CSU vet school—to its renowned cancer surgeon I am now aware of—for biopsy and evaluation at the outset. I am struggling with anger, feeling betrayed. In retrospect, there isn't a doubt in my mind that Dr. Gordon would have adamantly encouraged an immediate biopsy.

I await Dr. Villano's reply.

Physical assessment and statistics offer useful information, but they have limits. As a mother honors her inner knowing with a child, honoring my intuition was at least equally important. I was Maggie's caretaker and knew her better than anyone. My dreams repeatedly informed me *in advance* of logic and intellect. I just didn't get it. I struggle to stop blaming myself for tuning out my intuitive warnings.

I receive Dr. Villano's shocking reply. "We are holistic and dedicated to our views. CSU is ultra-aggressive, and in our mind, far too often performing experimental cancer therapies to the detriment of the animal. Thus, their perspective will be far different than ours."

I'm appalled to realize he advised me not from facts alone but also from his *beliefs* at our first appointment. I didn't know his personal biases about cancer therapies at that pivotal January appointment. We would not have put Maggie through an "ultra-aggressive" therapy. But did his beliefs prevent him from *considering* thyroid cancer or the potentially life-saving removal of a thyroid nodule? I'm learning it's not such an unusual canine diagnosis. My distress at learning his bias is similar to what I experienced in my dream, where he was practicing inappropriately.

It should have been *our* decision to make, not *his*.

As a health professional, I consider myself more holistic than traditional in my practice. Yet I believe a marriage of Western medicine and alternative approaches can offer people the best of both worlds. I never imagined I would receive anything less than *objective* options and information from Dr. Villano so that Tom and I, Maggie's guardians, could make a well-informed decision about her care. Objectivity is what all of us count on from any health provider. A crucial part of their jobs is to *inform* their patients in an unbiased manner of available treatments. If a professional has his own opinion and bias regarding treatment, I think it's fine, as long as it's presented that way.

I had doubts when I first recognized Dr. Villano in November of 2000. I needed to heed them and didn't. Then my dreams warned me he wouldn't know what was wrong with Maggie. If I understood at the time the predictive value of my dreams and how they tried to guide me, I'd have realized Dr. Villano was not the person for Maggie and me. Did his bias prevent him from strongly recommending that Maggie have a biopsy?

Certainly we count on veterinarians to diagnose and treat our animals' health problems. But I encourage you to bring your intuition to the table when you consult an expert. Don't discount it. Be aware of the parts your own fear and denial play. Keep in mind that experts can be wrong—that no one knows your animal like you do. The same is true with our family members. Trust yourself and your body messages. Intuition doesn't lie.

Chapter Sixteen
Profound Grief

I check the little Tupperware nest that holds the baby tree
swallows. They are feathered and grown-up looking. They
will fly any day. To think that Maggie's nose touched them
ever so gently at the beginning of their lives, and now she is
gone. Somehow they are a thread to her.

Sometimes special beings come into our lives and touch our
hearts in a way that leaves us forever changed. For me, Maggie
was such a special one. When my little princess died, it cast a
shadow on my own light. A chapter ended. The familiar road
we took together came to an abrupt end. Tom and I are in

uncharted territory without a map. Lost. Little do I know that Maggie's illness and death is our initiation into the next phase of our lives—that of caring for our declining elderly parents, of saying good-bye to them.

Being without Maggie is an aching, unbearable grief; tears search me out daily. When I look back, my dreams are so obvious now. Because I missed such important messages about Maggie, my grief is intensified. We can't get out of the house fast enough those first several mornings. We don't care where we go. Anywhere but in the emptiness of our home, where Maggie's absence screams from the hallways that once exploded with her aliveness. The world looks so different. I watch people laughing and enjoying themselves, but I'm disconnected from that foreign world, in a place far away. Blank. How am I going to live the rest of my life without her? Maggie was part of my soul.

Cinnamon is so much more affectionate. She waits for us at the top of the stairs when we come home. She even begins crossing her paws when she lies down the way Maggie always did. I sense her trying to fill in the gap, to take care of us. I notice her stare longingly at the memorial I created for Maggie. I pick Cinnamon up and place her among Maggie's things. She rubs against Maggie's dish; smells her harness; lies on the toys I placed in Maggie's dish. I'm thoroughly choked up, having never witnessed such an intimate animal scene. Her pupils widen when she sees Maggie's picture. She gets up and looks behind the picture. I know she misses Maggie. I explain to her again what happened, that Maggie won't be back. I get the sense Cinnamon is saying good-bye to Maggie in her own way.

Strangers we meet surprise me in the way they reach out, at times more than family and friends. They know. Those who experienced the loss of their own pets open their understanding, compassionate hearts to me in ways that offer the comfort of human connection and healing.

My mother surprises me with the tender compassion she expresses. She really gets it that Maggie was like my child and how special our relationship was. It opens a door of tenderness between us that has been closed for years. I am deeply touched.

My friend Judith gives of herself and her time so generously. She listens and is present in a way many people don't know how to be. In this, she gives us a gift of immeasurable value. Her caring heart helps us through.

With the above exceptions, I often feel alone with my loss. Some people may just not know what to do. Speaking to me in a cheery voice as though nothing happened makes it so much harder, creating greater distance between us. They mean well, but "have a great weekend" or "I hope all is well" makes me feel sad and more isolated with my loss, as though they don't have a clue as to the depth of my pain. Rather than ignore the subject, I need people to *talk* about Maggie, to ask me about her life, our relationship, her illness, and how we said good-bye. The silence around her name makes it as though she never existed and exacerbates my emptiness. I need those close to me to express their recognition of how much she meant to me. It hurts to experience friends who can't simply listen, be present, and be compassionate with us in our grief. My heart screams, "How can I lose this deepest of bonds, this most precious of relationships, and not have the loss of it profoundly acknowledged by those who knew us?"

What many people may not realize is that the bond between humans and their animals can be deeper than their bonds with a loved human.[1] Many of us view our pets as our children, especially those of us who haven't born our own children. I actually spent most of my moments with Maggie, except at work. Our spouses don't even spend the constant amount of time at our sides that our animals do.

Many people experience this very special, deep bond with their animals. Pets don't hurt or disappoint us the way humans can. We may grow and change more in our human relationships, but our animals are a constant; they offer us unconditional love during the conflicting times in our human relationships. They provide a touchstone of stability and love when the ground of our relationships and our own beings seems to shift beneath us. Maggie never judged me, so I was more genuinely myself with her than with any human. Perhaps this is another gift from our furry friends, a safe place to be fully ourselves. Grief from this type of loss is exceptionally profound. Because this human-animal bond is so deep, the grieving process may take even longer than when losing a family member.[2]

There is no *best* way to get through the loss of a beloved pet. I talk to many others who loved and lost their cherished pets. The way through the grief process is different for everyone. For some, it works to get another pet right away. To fill the void. Others can't conceive of doing that; they see a new pet as an invasion of the space and bond shared with the deceased animal. Some who try to fill the void too soon find they resent the new pet. Then that new bond suffers.

To respect my grief, I set aside quiet time alone each day. I need to decrease demands from the outside world, to allow my deep pain to express and release. I sit in silence in nature, write in my journal, or cry.

It helps to nurture myself in small ways: a hike among wildflowers in the mountains, a massage, and a dinner with Judith in our cozy home. Tom and I hold each other, go to a movie, and find comfort in our quiet time together.

It is consoling to be with people who can handle my sadness. I stay away from friends for the time being who have to be upbeat and avoid the topic—to protect myself—or be with them in small doses.

Our culture allows negligible time and space to grieve our human losses, let alone our pet losses. Our jobs expect us to be back at it, productive within a few days. Friends and family want to see us be "fine" long before we are anything close to fine. They expect us to move on. Family and friends are well intentioned when they suggest we get another dog. But that can't fill the void Maggie left. We would never think of telling someone who just lost their child to have another baby. In time, perhaps; I have to get through enough of my grief in order to be fair to another dog.

In a world that may seem totally out of step with our grief, a pet-loss support group can be a small oasis. I discover one online and find it soothing to communicate with others in the same boat. Both of our local humane societies also offer pet-bereavement groups.

Tom and I are in a double bind. We can't even think of getting another dog at this point. Yet we are desperate to be around dog energy. We stop to interact with every dog we pass on hiking trails or in town. We go to the humane societies in Longmont and Boulder to visit the dogs or take them for walks. It's as though we are searching for the essence of Maggie somehow and hope we will magically find her there.

We plan our involvement with the Humane Society of Boulder Valley. They offer so many options: fostering dogs, taking a dog to weekly training classes to increase its chances of adoption, and rehabilitating under-socialized or abused animals both in the shelter and at home. We seek out a local Lab rescue group to begin fostering with. The coordinator suggests we give it some time. She had a few unfortunate experiences with people who just lost their dogs being unable to cope with having even a foster dog in their home. She is looking out for our emotional state.

We all have to face grief and loss eventually. It's one of the great equalizers in life. Because it is often such an intense pain, some people simply don't want to let the depth of *our* hurt in because it reminds them of their *own* vulnerability to loss. They, too, will someday be in our shoes. But for now, they imagine they can make us feel better by remaining cheerful, when in truth that is what makes *them* feel more comfortable around us. It's okay to keep some distance temporarily from those who need you to be fine for their sake, or who don't support you in your loss because in their eyes "it's just an animal." Be sure to find compassionate people to surround yourself with.

"Often when somebody has a strong bond with an animal, they grieve deeply when the animal dies," says John Edward, a medium who communicates with people who have passed. "They feel tremendous guilt and ask if they could have done more. But I tell people that animals leave us when we've learned the lesson that they were here to teach us."[3] This is a reassuring thought.

I am ready to discover more of myself; finally willing to let go of a career I previously thought I should keep pursuing because I put so much time into it. After many rejections of my health-article queries, I realize this is not my desired path either. I want to write more about my own experiences and those of others. I'm starting to speak my truth with more clarity in my relationships—to validate my needs and feelings—less concerned with offending another. Not that I want to, but it's no longer dictating my responses. Perhaps Maggie sensed the shift and knew it was time to move on. She was the catalyst that began the process of reconnecting me with my genuine self. Mission accomplished.

I check our Tupperware nest again. Empty. Oh, how life has its metaphors.

Chapter Seventeen
Angels in Disguise

"What are you going to do today?" Tom asks as he is leaving for work.

"I don't know." Now that is a reply he's not heard before. I always have a plan, a list that no one can cover in a day. Yet somehow I expected to. My list controlled my day, as though busyness measured my self-worth.

But now, to *be* fully present—with all of my senses to experience each moment—is becoming as important as what I *do*. My extreme drive to accomplish goals begins to melt into letting my heart guide me. I'm not advocating stopping participation in life. Quite the contrary. I'm trying to slow it all down long enough to stop accomplishing for the sake of accomplishing. I become more conscious of how *should* and *have to* run my life, and make room for those voices I have never heard or silenced long ago. My mind is quieting. I like the peace that comes with it.

Maggie's illness and death ripples the foundation of what I think my purpose in life is. In losing my best friend, I also lose my willingness to work in an unfulfilling career. What is left is the desire to excavate potential dreams buried under what society taught me to be. To bring forth who I came into the world to be and do. I suspect part of that has to do with animals, dogs in particular.

I sense the time I have been spending to update myself on the latest Western and alternative health information coming to a close. I'm not sure where my heart will lead, so

I give myself permission to explore. I consider working as a pet loss and bereavement counselor, but that passes. I'm attracted to learn whatever I can about dogs. That includes learning positive reinforcement techniques in dog training, volunteering with the Humane Society of Boulder Valley, and becoming a volunteer dog trainer with Freedom Service Dogs to train dogs for people with mobility impairments. I'd like to eventually use my nurse practitioner skills in a volunteer capacity—to simply treat patients—without the restrictions imposed by HMOs. I love to sing, even though I don't have a good voice; maybe I'll take voice lessons. I take a writing course.

Writing is a long-buried dream that life frequently reminded me of. First, my English Composition professor in college encouraged me to audit the class after reading my impromptu essay he instructed the class to write on the first day of the semester. He said my writing skills were beyond what the class offered. The second event occurred a few years later in an airport, when the ticket agent repeated my name and said, "*Hmm*, sounds like the name of a famous author." He stopped me in my tracks. Finally, when I had a psychic reading a few years ago, she emphasized that I absolutely had to write in this lifetime; that it's in all my *houses*—an astrology term I don't really understand. I told her I was going to write factual health-oriented articles, that I knew I couldn't write a novel. She shook her head. "No, it will be something else—more creative—from your heart." I was sure she was dead wrong.

I do stop writing health—and dog-behavior articles. I begin to journal daily about my life with Maggie; it's the greatest comfort to my grieving heart, a way to stay connected with her. And to eventually conceive a book in her honor.

Tom and I take a weekend workshop in Tellington Touch, a technique that helps calm animals. It aids abused, neglected, or fearful animals. I speak with Ingrid at the seminar, a woman who does energy work with animals at the Longmont Humane Society.

"I believe our animals are so sensitive they often take on our issues for us," she says. "Our unresolved emotional problems can manifest as health problems in our pets."

Whoa. This is a hard one to wrap my arms around.

I read up on it some. According to Eastern religions, the human body contains seven chakras—energy centers—that are vertically aligned, running from the base of the spine to the crown of the head.[1] "As a person masters each chakra, he gains power and self-knowledge that becomes integrated into his spirit."[2] When a chakra is blocked or imbalanced, physical symptoms or illness may occur in that area of the body. The fifth chakra contains the throat, neck, and *thyroid gland.*[3] Emotional issues with this chakra include personal expression, following one's dream, using personal power to create, and the capacity to make decisions.[4] Can it really be that Maggie reflected blocks and imbalances in *my* creativity, personal power, and expression—my biggest lessons—through *her* thyroid cancer? That is pretty painful to swallow.

If Maggie's illness did represent my own areas of being stuck, I owe it to her as well as myself to bring forth my dreams and a fuller, more genuine me in my relationships. That may mean letting go of the need to please others and not always agreeing with others. Disagreement wasn't an option in my family of origin. It also means recognizing darker feelings, like anger and depression—to learn their messages—rather than stifle them. Having been raised by a mother who lived in her dark feelings much of the time, the rest of our family exaggerated the positive and suppressed our dark sides. I'm working on the balance, realizing we need darkness in order for light to shine. When we prohibit what are typically called negative feelings from being expressed in ourselves and others, they can become even more dominant. As Maggie loved me with all my flaws, I begin to love Mom for the caring, sensitive person she is under her difficult exterior behaviors. I also discover the part I played in resisting who she was.

I become much more conscious of the root and extent of my restrictive self-expression. I focused previous therapy sessions on my relationship with my parents. Now I begin to discover that the communication patterns between my family and me that are dysfunctional and invalidating go beyond my mom and dad. I'm afraid to give direct, candid responses if I sense they will lead to disapproval or humiliation by family members. So I often withhold frank responses. I see now how this dysfunctional pattern held me back in many areas of my life. As I cease participating in this unhealthy pattern, I realize how thin the line is that I walk with my family. What I didn't see yet was that it would soon cost me three very dear relationships for several excruciating years.

Tim, a massage therapist who works on my body during my agonizing family conflict, puts both hands up to his throat. "I just feel like you're so stuck here, like you want to speak and can't." I flash back on the toxic cancer taking over Maggie's throat. Was Tim's astute perception a validation that my soul companion showed me, in her death, what I needed to heal in order to fully live? If so, our animals give us even more than I ever considered before.

I come to appreciate that animals are here on our planet for humans. As Maggie did for me, dogs bring us into the present, to find joy in the moment as they do, and to love unconditionally. Even as their bodies begin to fail, they find joy as Maggie did almost to her last day.

My relationship with my black beauty helped me peel layers from my long-protected heart and take emotional risks with significant people in my life. Our journey together awakened me to dreams as a means of communication between our spirits, as messages from the soul. It taught me to question the premise that humans are more advanced beings than animals. Are we? Or are we simply different yet equal beings, all here on our own spiritual journeys? Dogs love unconditionally and remind us to do the same. What an interesting coincidence that *d-o-g* is *G-o-d* spelled backwards in the English language.

According to John Edward, a psychic medium, "Animals are God's little helpers. They're here to guide us, to walk us through life as a reminder of what we're all here to learn: what unconditional love really is. Animals are already highly evolved before they come into a physical presence ... People must be aware that this is a priceless energy. Animals ... all animals, are a gift from God and they must be treated as such."[5] They are our angels in disguise given to us to guide us on our paths and teach us on life's journey.

I go out to our elevated bedroom deck and sit down. In front of me is the familiar sight of tree swallows dipping from the sky to grab insects. Movement catches my eye from a limb of our characteristic dead tree in the backyard. I move closer to the railing. Can it be? Lined up on the limb are three smaller versions of the swallows I saw a moment ago. One by one, they dip after the adult birds. Our babies haven't left after all. Mom and Dad are teaching them to hunt. Ah, the thread continues. Life goes on.

Chapter Eighteen
Beyond Our Five Senses

*B*y this time, my red salvia flowers that were reduced to stubs by the snowstorm are flaming red, lush, fuller and brighter than ever before. My impatiens flowers are colorful and full—a true rebirth. I am struck by the cycle of death and resurrection that occurs every spring and fall in nature.

I've gravitated toward a belief in reincarnation for many years. It makes the most sense to me when I think of the varied and unequal circumstances we are born into all over the planet.

Years ago, I stepped out of the familiar parameters of the Christian religion I was raised with. I explored Judaism and Eastern religions, which allowed me to significantly broaden my spiritual views. I learned that Buddhists and Hindus believe that humans reincarnate after death, that different lives offer us new lessons to learn to evolve to a higher consciousness. Eastern religions believe that our spirits come back to earth in *many* lifetimes. Some believe that spirits often return to their same families to experience different relationships. I was quite surprised to discover that prior to modern Christianity, early Christians also believed in reincarnation.

The truth is, we don't know intellectually if human or animal spirits live on after death. Most religions teach us that our spirits go on to another realm, or to heaven. But religious institutions don't address what happens to the souls of our beloved pets.

I am surprised to discover friends and others in my life who believe animal spirits live on as ours are believed to after we pass from this world. They believe our pets can and do choose to return after they die, that they come into this life to learn lessons just as we do. What a concept. Will Maggie come back to me? Or is this just magical thinking?

"I have this feeling that our special animal friends find their way back to us after they pass on," writes Jeanette on her sympathy card.

"Why not wait for a reincarnated Maggie?" quips Mike, Tom's friend, when I share how sad and empty I feel without her.

"You will find her," says Jarrett sweetly, our four-year-old neighbor girl who regularly played with Maggie at the lake. This is her first experience with death. Ah, out of the mouths of babes....

"Call her back to you," encourages Theresa, my dream therapist.

Is this possible?

"I have a feeling that my Labrador, Dinah, is my very special dog from my twenties, reincarnated," ventures Pam, a nurse-practitioner colleague of mine. "There are even strong physical resemblances, even though they are different breeds." This is a real shocker to hear coming from my very scientifically minded colleague.

Jaison is a man convinced that his fourteen-year-old dog,

Shannon, who recently died, was the reincarnated spirit of his previous dog, who died when hit by a car at age ten.

"How did you find her again?" I inquire. I'm quite astonished at the numbers of people I'm having animal-reincarnation conversations with.

"I had a dream and a woman's voice announced that Shannon was coming back," he replies. "Then I just knew it. Intuition guided me to a particular breeder I knew of. When I saw her in the litter, I knew immediately it was her, with the help of a psychic friend of mine."

"She's done here now. She's not coming back," said Jaison. "I can feel that her spirit has moved on. I don't feel her around me like I did last time."

Hmm. The limits of my belief system are being challenged as I entertain this novel concept.

"Why don't you speak with an animal communicator?" Judith suggests. "I did when Sheeba died, and it really gave me peace of mind." The animal communicator told Judith her dog, Sheeba, was an advanced soul and didn't need to come back to learn lessons on earth anymore. Judith gives me the name of the woman she spoke with.

I have never heard of animal communicators before. Skeptically, I dial the phone and make the appointment with Joan. She asks me to send a picture of Maggie, along with basic information including her age, how long we had her, and how she died.

Several days go by, and I have my telephone appointment with Joan. She mentions several things that are so accurate about Maggie's personality. But I'm not prepared when she says, "You know, Maggie was in your life once before, for a very brief time when you were a young child. She was a very young dog, less than four months old, and she was hit by a car."

My mouth drops open. I nearly fall out of my chair. She is

describing our beagle pup, Foxy. When I was seven, I watched in horror as he was hit by a car in front of our house and subsequently died in our garage surrounded by my entire family.

Foxy gave me my first lesson in death and loss, my first broken heart. He was a dear, sweet soul who lived with us only briefly before his untimely death. Forty-one years later, Maggie's death initiates me into the next phase of my life. I am about to enter the years of caring for my aging and declining parents, closer than I know to saying good-bye to them.

Everything she said about Foxy is true. We only had him for one month. He was about four months old. I reel from the accuracy of her information.

"You and Maggie have been together in many lifetimes before," she softly informs me. This is an introduction to spiritual possibilities I never considered.

"She'll serve you better in spirit form over the next year than she would in a body," Joan tells me. "Call on her."

I suddenly remember Maggie's unexplained broken sternum. The mystery of how it happened faded into the background—given the gravity of her condition when Dr. Crystal discovered it—until now. What a strange discovery at the end of her life. She never had an injury to warrant breaking her sternum. I share this story with Joan.

"Sometimes animals, like humans, come back with weaknesses in the areas of their bodies that relate to their death in a past life. It may have taken only a minor trauma to break her sternum if it was broken when she was hit by a car in a previous life," Joan says.

Joan also lets me know that Maggie didn't want the surgery to remove her thyroid nodule. "She didn't want to die an old dog. Maggie wanted to go out with her spark, her aliveness."

I really believe this is true about Maggie. I never could imagine her as an old dog. Could there have been an unconscious communication between Maggie and Dr. Villano at that first appointment that set our chosen path in motion? I also entertain the possibility that Maggie may not have survived surgery to remove the nodule, had we done so back in January. Perhaps we had her six months longer than we would have. These thoughts put an entirely different twist on my perceptions. They ease my guilt *and* my anger toward Dr. Villano.

My relationship with Maggie is what opened my mind to the possibility of psychic communication between animals and humans. If psychics can read people, and psychic mediums can communicate with people who have passed, why wouldn't they also be capable of communication with animals both here and on the other side? Some humans appear to be much more open and sensitive to psychic phenomenon. Do psychics and animal communicators have that *sixth sense* that most of us have but never develop, or lose as a child because the adults in their world don't believe in or foster perceptions that children share?

Marta Williams believes the ability exists in all of us to intuitively communicate with nature and animals. It's "the first language, the foundation of spoken and written words, and the common link between all species."[1]

My dreams tell me Maggie's spirit is still here. Since she passed, I feel her presence around me so strongly at times. These are the moments when I know there's more to this world than what we experience with our limited five senses. Can it be that the spirit world is right here, but most of us lack the extrasensory abilities to perceive it?

Chapter Nineteen
What One Dog Can Do

I sit on the deck meditating under the shade of our pine trees. Hummingbirds fill the skies with their music. The sweet dream I had in South Padre Island during Maggie's last trip there—with the many foster puppies in Madonna's garage licking my face—floats into memory.

Madonna is our neighbor who fostered puppies and kittens for the Longmont Humane Society for many years. Was this dream a foreshadowing of the stream of rescue dogs that are to grace our lives after Maggie's passing? Our love for Maggie turns outward to dogs in need. We train dogs at the Humane Society of Boulder Valley (HSBV) to assist them in becoming more adoptable. We undertake the challenge to work with under-socialized dogs to help them build trust in humans, one small step at a time. A handful of energetic Labrador retrievers from Front Range Labrador Rescue find there "forever" homes after a foster stay in our home, as do other HSBV dogs.

It's Saturday, late morning. I finish an HSBV training class with Manny, an unruly Labrador and shepherd mix. He is coming along, finally allowing touch. He shied away from it until now, unable to relate well with humans. I breathe a little easier knowing his beginning ability to relate means there is hope for him to be adopted.

I head for Mount Sanitas for a little exercise. I'm walking alone on the Valley Trail and can still envision Maggie at my side. I come upon a man training and treating his white shepherd. I comment on how well his dog responds to his commands.

He smiles. "When I was a kid, we went and got a couple of dogs from the pound and threw them in the backyard, and that was it. Today, it's different. You train them. You understand each other. She lives in the house and goes on vacation with us."

Yes, it is different today. I believe we are on the brink of a paradigm shift, finally learning what animals, especially dogs, are capable of. We're beginning to see them as the intelligent, emotional beings they are. For years, they have assisted the physically, mentally, and emotionally challenged as service dogs. Some can alert epileptics to an impending seizure. Canines assist our military in wars. They are a vital part of search-and-rescue teams. Dogs have been known to jump into bodies of water to save loved ones and strangers alike. Some even alert mothers when their infants have stopped breathing in their cribs. Dogs are used therapeutically with prisoners, the elderly, the ill, and with high-risk teenagers. They are being used for their exquisite sense of smell to detect cancer in humans. We are realizing dogs do think and perhaps pick up our intentions and emotions in a way we don't yet understand.

My heart is open with love and hope for Manny and the many shelter dogs like him. I can feel Maggie's spirit, and I feel full. The dogs I meet on the trail run up to greet me, to receive affectionate pets. It's as though the love I shared with Maggie was so large that it can no longer be contained in one dog-human bond anymore, but overflows to all dogs that cross my path, and their humans, too.

Words from a Garth Brooks song run through my head:

If tomorrow never comes
Will she know how much I loved her?
Is the love I gave her in the past

Going to be enough to last
If tomorrow never comes?[1]

Yes, my beloved Maggie, it was enough. I know how much you loved me. And I hope you know, my precious princess, how much I will always love you.

Months later, Maggie comes to me in a dream:

Maggie's in the kitchen with the baby gate up. She's looking at me and communicates to me without words, "I am coming on another trip." Then I'm in the kitchen with Maggie, and a puppy is there with her. I'm so happy she's here. I want to hug her, spend my time with her, but I have to tend to the puppy. Maggie is watching me and the pup, patiently staying in the background....

Epilogue

*T*om and I are finally blessed with that grandchild. Our beautiful grandson, Aaron, was born on January 7, 2006, to Tom and Fabiola. It was the day of my mother's memorial service. Another affirmation of the cycle of life. He adds an entirely new delight to our lives.

We can only place Scott in the hands of a higher power. We hope that somehow, he will find enough self-love to choose life.

As old patterns and relationships unraveled, I came to experience a newfound freedom in my body and soul—of course that was *after* I picked up my broken pieces and put myself back together again like Humpty Dumpty. I am more genuine. The resulting self-love opened doors to greater love and compassion for others. Family relationships eventually came together in new ways and found a healthier balance.

Indeed, I did find dog love again. After a year of fostering numerous dogs, it was time. We were both drawn to golden retrievers. A voice inside kept repeating, "Adopt an older dog." That was a big step from, "I'll *never get* another dog." Tom was on the same page. We somehow thought we wouldn't get so attached. Oh, silly us.

We adopted Chloe from Golden Retriever Rescue of the Rockies. She was eleven years old. Her family had moved to Peru. Chloe's grief was written all over her soft, white face. It happens more than you might believe. Older dogs that have lived their entire lives with someone are taken to humane societies and rescue groups for reasons as numerous as dog breeds. They have the hardest time being adopted, because people generally want younger dogs for the obvious reasons. If you can find it in your heart, adopt one.

For Tom, the bond was immediate. It took me awhile. Of course, when it came, it was a very different bond than what I had with Maggie, but special in its own way. Chloe had been a backyard dog. We wanted to give her the best rest of her life possible. With Chloe, it was about us giving to her. She had numerous health problems. We thought we'd be lucky to have her for a year. What an amazing, tenacious spirit. Chloe trained to become a therapy dog, and we became a team at Sunrise Assisted Living Center. She walked by our sides through some of our darkest days of parent loss and family conflict, and she became our own personal therapy dog. Sensitive, sweet Queen Chloe graced our lives for three-and-a-half years before she succumbed to lymphoma.

I did begin those voice lessons, along with several vocal performance classes. I even performed several solos on stage. Not in my wildest dreams did I see this coming. It was Maggie who led me to find my voice, but poor Chloe is the one who sat through the lessons and the classes!

We only waited three months this time. Having also lost both sets of our parents and a close friend within two years, life seemed a luxury we now knew to be precious and brief. Too many dogs, too little time. It was going to be a yellow Lab this time. I plugged in our criteria on the Denver Dumb Friends League Web site: Labrador, female, one year old or younger. The link took me to the Denver Municipal Animal Shelter site. There she was. I did a double-take. She sat in her picture as Maggie did in our kitchen behind the baby gate when she was young, and as she did in my dream. A precious *black* face. So much for the yellow Lab. We went to see her that day. She was picked up on the streets by animal control—even had tags—but the owner relinquished her. The shelter estimated her to be ten months of age. She greeted us like she'd known us forever. This one *had it*—what no other Lab we met since Maggie died had—joy and exuberance even as dogs charged her aggressively from their kennels. That "the world is my oyster" attitude. Energy to burn. Smart and responsive.

Maddie, short for Magdalene, taxed our resources with her lack of training and tendency to run off when we first adopted her. But training and patience paid off. What a wonderful, devoted girl she is. She even loves to cuddle, once her energy is burned. At just over two-and-a-half years old, she again fills our home with her happy spirit and aliveness. And Cinnamon once more has a buddy to sleep with. Oh, and to travel with. Yes, at the ripe age of fourteen, Cinnamon's late-life adventures include summer mountain camping trips and watching the ocean in South Padre Island. Her favorite part is cuddling with Maddie in the backseat of the truck during the long drive down.

Endnotes

Chapter Two

1. Pryor, *Don't Shoot the Dog*, 1.

2. Baer and Duno, *Leader of the Pack*, xiii–xviii.

3. Pivar and Nelson, *Taking Care of Puppy Business: A Gentle Approach for Positive Results*, 25.

4. Baer and Duno, *Leader of the Pack*, 61–62.

Chapter Three

1. Boone, *Kinship With All Life*, 35.

2. Chopra, *Creating Health*, 85–86.

3. Fekete, "Gift from God," *Santa Maria Times*, December 24, 2001, B1.

4. Ivin-Amar, "Carl Gustav Jung on Dreams, From Dreams to Self Understanding," http://www.spiritcommunity.com/dreams/jung/php.

Chapter Five

1. Wikipedia, the Free Encyclopedia, "Ropes Course," http://en.wikipedia.org/wiki/Ropes_course.

2. University of Buffalo, "Pet-Owning Couples Are Closer, Interact More Than Pet-Less Couples, UB Study Shows," news release, February 27, 1998.

Chapter Nine

1. Puotinen, *The Encyclopedia of Natural Pet Care*, 289.

2. Pitcairn and Pitcairn, *Dr. Pitcairn's Complete Guide to Natural Health for Dogs and Cats*, 235.

3. Pitcairn and Pitcairn, *Dr. Pitcairn's Complete Guide to Natural Health for Dogs and Cats*, 10–12.

4. Pitcairn and Pitcairn, *Dr. Pitcairn's Complete Guide to Natural Health for Dogs and Cats*, 16.

5. Pitcairn and Pitcairn, *Dr. Pitcairn's Complete Guide to Natural Health for Dogs and Cats*, 9.

6. Pitcairn and Pitcairn, *Dr. Pitcairn's Complete Guide to Natural Health for Dogs and Cats*, 19.

7. Hurburgh, Iowa State University Extension, Mycotoxins in the Grain Market," http://www.extension.iastate.edu/grain/info/mycotoxinsinthegrainmarket.htm.

8. Pitcairn and Pitcairn, *Dr. Pitcairn's Complete Guide to Natural Health for Dogs and Cats*, 16.

9. Pitcairn and Pitcairn, *Dr. Pitcairn's Complete Guide to Natural Health for Dogs and Cats*, 17.

10. U.S. Department of Health and Human Services, Public Health Service, National Toxicology Program, Report on Carcinogens, Eleventh Edition, "Butylated Hydroxyanisole (BHA) CAS No. 25013-16-5," http://ntp.niehs.nih.gov/ntp/roc/eleventh/profiles/s027bha.pdf

11. FDA Center for Veterinary Medicine, "CVM Update, FDA Requests that Ethoxyquin Levels Be Reduced in Dog

Foods," http://www.fda.gov/cvm/CVM__Updates/dogethox.
html.

12. Puotinen, *The Encyclopedia of Natural Pet Care,* 216.

13. Pitcairn and Pitcairn, *Dr. Pitcairn's Complete Guide to Natural Health for Dogs and Cats,* 116–117.

14. Pitcairn and Pitcairn, *Dr. Pitcairn's Complete Guide to Natural Health for Dogs and Cats,* 323-325.

15. Pitcairn and Pitcairn, *Dr. Pitcairn's Complete Guide to Natural Health for Dogs and Cats,* 323-324.

16. Pitcairn and Pitcairn, *Dr. Pitcairn's Complete Guide to Natural Health for Dogs and Cats,* 323–324.

17. Pitcairn and Pitcairn, *Dr. Pitcairn's Complete Guide to Natural Health for Dogs and Cats,* 247.

Chapter Eleven

1. Kaplan, *Dreams Are Letters From the Soul,* 113, 123.

2. Ivin-Amar, "Carl Gustav Jung on Dreams, From Dreams to Self Understanding," http://www.spiritcommunity.com/dreams/jung/php.

Chapter Thirteen

1. Duda, "Thyroid Cancer in Dogs," http://www.oncolink.upenn.edu/experts/article.cfm?c=3&s=32&ss=86&id=1294.

2. NC State College of Veterinary Medicine, Department of Clinical Sciences, "Oncology, Thyroid Carcinoma in Dogs," http://www.cvm.ncsu.edu/docs/onco/thyroidcarcinoma__dogs.html.

Chapter Fourteen

1. Ross, *On Death and Dying,* 93.

Chapter Fifteen

1. Williams, *Beyond Words: Talking with Animals and Nature,* 3–4.

2. Williams, *Beyond Words: Talking with Animals and Nature,* 3.

Chapter Sixteen

1. Sife, *The Loss of a Pet,* 5–6.

2. Sife, *The Loss of a Pet,* 9.

3. Richard, *The Message Is The Medium,* 22.

Chapter Seventeen

1. Myss, *Anatomy of the Spirit,* 68.

2. Myss, *Anatomy of the Spirit,* 68.

3. Myss, *Anatomy of the Spirit,* 98.

4. Myss, *Anatomy of the Spirit,* 99.

5. Richard, *The Message Is the Medium,* 22.

Chapter Eighteen

1. Williams, *Beyond Words: Talking with Animals and Nature,* 3.

Chapter Nineteen

1. Brooks, *Garth Brooks,* track three, compact disc.

Reference Guide

Humane Organizations

American Society for the Prevention of Cruelty to Animals
424 East 92nd Street
New York, NY 10128-6804
Phone: 212-876-7700
http://www.aspca.org

Best Friends Animal Sanctuary
(A large no-kill refuge for abandoned and abused animals)
5001 Angel Canyon
Kanab, UT 84741-5000
Phone: 435-644-2001
http://www.bestfriends.org

Humane Society of Boulder Valley (HSBV)
2323 55th St.
Boulder, CO 80301
Phone: 303-442-4030
http://boulderhumane.org

Longmont Humane Society
9595 Nelson Road
Longmont, CO 80501
Phone: 303-772-1232
http://longmonthumane.org

Safe Harbor Lab Rescue
601 16th St., #C-322
Golden, CO 80401

Phone: 303-464-7777
http://www.safeharborlabrescue.org

The Humane Society of the United States
2100 L Street, NW
Washington, DC 20037
Phone: 202-452-1100
http://www.hsus.org

Humane Charities

(The Humane Charity Seal of Approval is the easiest way for donors to identify charities that advance medical research without the use of animals.)
Humane Charity Seal of Approval
Melanie Hiller
5100 Wisconsin Avenue, N.W.
Suite 400
Washington, DC 20016
Phone: 202-686-2210, ext. 369
http://www.HumaneSeal.org

Training Organizations

The Association of Pet Dog Trainers
150 Executive Center Drive, Box 35
Greenville, SC 29615
Phone: 1-800-PET-DOGS
http://www.apdt.com

HSBV Training and Behavior Center
2323 55th St.
Boulder, CO 80301
Phone: 303-442-4030
http://boulderhumane.org

Medical Alert Dog Organizations

Dogs4Diabetics, Inc.
1647 Willow Pass Road, #157
Concorde, CA 94520-2611
http://www.dogs4diabetics.com

Carolina Canines for Service, Inc.
(Trains dogs to alert for seizures)
P.O. Box 12643
Wilmington, NC 28405
Toll-free phone: 866-910-3647
http://www.seizureassistdogs.org

Therapy Dogs

Therapy Dogs Inc.
P.O. Box 5868
Cheyenne, WY 82003
Phone: 877-843-7364
http://therapydogs.com

Pet Loss

http://www.petloss.com
(Lists pet-loss support groups by state)

Animal Communicators

Joan Ranquet
Harmony Farm, Duvall, Washington
Phone: 425-788-3888
888-882-7208 V.M.
http://www.joanranquet.com

Bibliography

Baer, Nancy, and Steve Duno. *Leader of the Pack*. New York: HarperCollins Publishers, 1996.

Boone, J. Allen. *Kinship With All Life*. New York: HarperCollins Publishers, 1954.

Brooks, Garth. *Garth Brooks*. "If Tomorrow Never Comes." Compact disc. Cond. Garth Brooks. Comp. Capitol Records. © 1989.

Chopra, Deepak. *Creating Health*. Boston: Houghton Mifflin Company, 1991.

Duda, Lila. "Thyroid Cancer in Dogs." *OncoLinkVet, Abramson Cancer Center of the University of Pennsylvania*. November 1, 2001. http://www.oncolink.upenn.edu/experts/article.cfm?c=3&s=32&ss=86&id=1294 (accessed September 26, 2007).

Fekete, Britt. "Gift From God." *Santa Maria Times*. December 24, 2001: B1.

Hurburgh, Jr., CR. "Mycotoxins in the Grain Market." *Iowa State University Extension; Iowa Grain Quality Initiative*. 2008. http://www.extension.iastate.edu/grain/info/mycotoxinsinthegrainmarket.htm (accessed January 17, 2008).

Ivin-Amar, Silvana. "Carl Gustav Jung on Dreams, From Dreams to Self Understanding." SpiritCommunity.com.

http://www.spiritcommunity.com/dreams/jung/php. (accessed September 20, 2007).

Kaplan, Connie. *Dreams Are Letters From The Soul.* New York: Harmony Books, 2002.

Myss, Caroline. *Anatomy of the Spirit: The Seven Stages of Power and Healing.* New York: Harmony Books, 1996.

NC State University College of Veterinary Medicine, Department of Clinical Sciences. "Oncology, Thyroid Carcinoma in Dogs." *NC State University College of Veterinary Medicine.* http://www.cvm.ncsu.edu/docs/onco/thyroidcarcinoma_dogs.html (accessed September 24, 2007).

Pitcairn, Richard H., and Susan H. Pitcairn. *Dr. Pitcairn's Complete Guide to Natural Health for Dogs & Cats.* Emmaus: Rodale Press, Inc., 1995.

Pivar, Gail, and Leslie Nelson. *Taking Care of Puppy Business: A Gentle Approach for Positive Results.* South Elgin: Tails-U-Win!, 1998.

Pryor, Karen. *Don't Shoot The Dog.* New York: Bantam Books, 1999.

Richard, Julie. "The Message Is the Medium!" *Best Friends Magazine,* November/December 2001: 22.

Ross, Elizabeth K. *On Death and Dying.* New York: Macmillan Publishing Company, 1969.

Sife, Wallace. *The Loss of a Pet.* New York: Howell Book House, 1998.

University of Buffalo. "Pet-Owning Couples Are Closer, Interact More Than Pet-Less Couples, UB study shows." News release. February 27, 1998. http://www.eureka-lert.org/pub__releases/1998-02/UaB-PCAC-270298.php (accessed September 5, 2007).

U.S. Department of Health and Human Services, Public Health Service, National Toxicology Program. "Substance Profiles, Butylated Hydroxyanisole (BHA) CAS No. 25013-16-5." *Report on Carcinogens, Eleventh Edition: Butylated Hydroxyanisole (BHA).* http://ntp.niehs.nih.gov/ntp/roc/eleventh/profiles/s027bha.pdf (accessed January 17, 2008).

U.S Food and Drug Administration, Center for Veterinary Medicine. *CVM Update, FDA Requests That Ethoxyquin Levels Be Reduced in Dog Foods.* (August 14, 1997). http://www.fda.gov/cvm/CVM__Updates/dogethox.   html (accessed January 17, 2008).

Wikipedia, the Free Encyclopedia. "Ropes Course." http://en.wikipedia.org/wiki/Ropes__course (accessed September 1, 2007).

Williams, Marta. *Beyond Words: Talking With Animals and Nature.* Novato: New World Library, 2005.

About the Author

Dawn Kairns is a Family Nurse Practitioner and has published in nursing journals and *American Fitness Magazine.* A life-long animal lover, her passion for dogs led her to volunteer with several local animal rescue organizations, and in the aftermath of Hurricane Katrina, the Humane Society of the United States. Dawn lives in Boulder, Colorado, with her husband, Tom, and their dog, Maddie, and cat, Cinnamon. Visit www.dawnkairns.com

978-0-595-47435-6
0-595-47435-7